THE SIMPSONS

FAMILY HISTORY

A CELEBRATION OF TELEVISION'S FAVORITE FAMILY

MATT GROENING

ABRAMS, NEW YORK

Acknowledgments

This book would not have been possible without the contributions of the many talented writers, artists, and actors who have lent their prodigious abilities to *The Simpsons* and shaped it into one of the most successful and beloved television shows in history.

THE SIMPSONS FAMILY HISTORY
By Matt Groening

Writing: Nathan Kane
Book Design and Layout: Serban Cristescu
Editorial: Terry Delegeane
Production: Christopher Ungar
Production Assistance: Art Villanueva, Pete Benson
Art: Chia-Hsien Jason Ho, Mike Rote
Research: Karen Bates, Max Davison, Nathan Hamill, Ruth Waytz, Robert Zaugh

Special thanks to: Susan A. Grode, Mili Smythe, Bill Morrison,
Deanna MacLellan, Ursula Wendel, Vyolet N. Diaz

Production Manager: Anet Sirna-Bruder

Library of Congress Control Number: 2014930727

ISBN: 978-1-4197-1399-6

Printed and bound in the United States
10 9 8 7 6 5 4 3 2 1

THE ART OF BOOKS SINCE 1949

115 West 18th Street
New York, NY 10011
www.abramsbooks.com

THE SIMPSONS™

FAMILY HISTORY

A CELEBRATION OF TELEVISION'S FAVORITE FAMILY

MATT GROENING

The Simpsons are family to me.

I've been doodling misshapen, bulgy-eyed cartoon characters with tragic overbites since the sixth grade. Somehow I grew up and found myself in a Hollywood-style, movie studio bungalow on the 20th Century Fox lot in Los Angeles, pitching this quickly sketched family (with names borrowed from my *real live action* family) for a series of animated short films. That was almost thirty years ago.

What happened next is a whirlwind of some fifty-odd animated shorts, five-hundred-and-fifty-plus episodes over twenty-six seasons (and counting), one feature film, a dozen video games, a couple breakfast cereals, and a phenomenon that has spread across the globe in everything from pirated DVDs to bootleg piñatas.

Millions (billions?) of people have watched the Simpsons grow up for a quarter of a century. And by grow up I mean stay pretty much the same. Of course, Homer and Marge never age, Lisa and Bart are forever stuck in the second and fourth grades, respectively, and Maggie will never outgrow that blue onesie or lose that soggy pacifier. But that doesn't mean there wasn't a beginning to the never-ending Simpsons saga. Homer and Marge had their first meet-cute, first date, first kiss, and first (of many) weddings. Bart pulled his first prank, caused his first international scandal, and got beaten up the first (of many) times. Lisa blew her first saxophone solo, staged her first protest, and had her first (of many) disappointments. And Maggie spoke her first word (albeit in private).

That's my family history, and I'm guessing that's your family history, too. As the whole Simpson story has trundled along, just like your own life, you've been there. Or you were born after the Simpsons debuted, in which case you have a lot of catching up to do.

So let's get underway with the unvarnished, unabridged, unexpurgated, and altogether straightforward and chronological chronicles of Our Favorite Family.

Your pal (and honorary weird uncle),

MATT GROENING

SPROUTING FROM INAUSPICIOUS BEGINNINGS, THE
SIMPSON FAMILY HAS A LONG AND VARIED HISTORY.
THE ONLY CONSTANT AMONG FAMILY MEMBERS SEEMS TO
BE A GENERAL LACK OF REFINEMENT AND QUESTIONABLE
CHARACTER TRAITS. IN OTHER WORDS...

"THEY'RE TERRIBLE!"

–LISA SIMPSON

"YEAH, THE SIMPSON FAMILY IS A LONG LINE OF HORSE THIEVES, DEADBEATS, HORSE BEATS, DEAD THIEVES, AND EVEN A FEW ALCOHOLICS."

—HOMER SIMPSON

SIMPSON STRIKES AGAIN

"OUR ANCESTORS WERE EVEN KICKED OUT OF AUSTRALIA."

—ABE SIMPSON

TO TRULY UNDERSTAND THEM, ONE MUST JOURNEY BACK INTO THE PAST.

IN THE BEGINNING...

A PROTEAN MIASMA SWIRLS
UPON THE EDGE OF EXISTENCE.

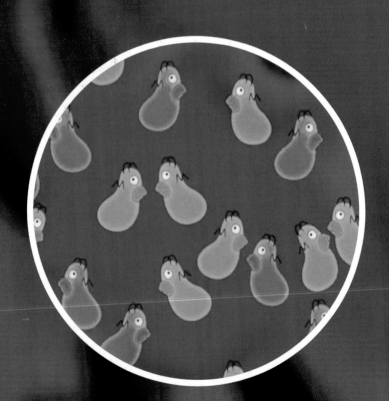

THE EMBRYONIC
BUILDING BLOCKS OF LIFE
CHURN AND REPLICATE
IN THE DARKNESS.

A NEW WORLD!

A HARSH ENVIRONMENT RULED BY COLOSSAL BEHEMOTHS,

WHERE THUNDERING BEASTS BATTLE FOR SUPREMACY...

AND THE WEAK BECOME FOOD FOR THE STRONG.

BUT NOTHING WITHSTANDS THE FIERY COMET WHICH FALLS FROM THE HEAVENS AND THREATENS TO

FROM THE DESK OF
MATT GROENING

WE ONLY HAVE SO MANY PAGES AVAILABLE, GUYS. DO WE REALLY NEED TO START AT THE DAWN OF TIME? LET'S PICK UP THE PACE A BIT.

THANKS!
MG

67 MILLION

YEARS LATER...

COMING TO AMERICA

ORVILLE SIMPSON, HIS YOUNGEST SON ABE, AND THE REST OF THE SIMPSON FAMILY LEAVE THE OLD COUNTRY AND SET SAIL FOR AMERICA.

"MY FATHER THOUGHT AMERICA WAS THE GREATEST THING SINCE SLICED BREAD.

SLICED BREAD HAVING BEEN INVENTED THE PREVIOUS WINTER."

—ABE

ARRIVING AT THE STATUE OF LIBERTY, FATHER AND SON SHARE A POIGNANT MOMENT.

"THERE IT IS. OUR NEW HOME."

THEY LIVE THERE A FEW MONTHS BUT ARE FORCED TO MOVE ONCE THE STATUE'S HEAD FILLS WITH GARBAGE.

TWENTIETH-CENTURY FACTS

ABE SIMPSON LIVES A COLORFUL LIFE IN HIS ADOPTED COUNTRY, FROM HIS HUMBLE BEGINNING AS A SHOESHINE BOY TO HIS INFAMOUS STINT AS A PROFESSIONAL ATHLETE IN THE WOMEN'S BASEBALL LEAGUE.

"I WAS A CENTER FIELDER FOR THE SPRINGFIELD FLOOZIES. THE PAY WASN'T MUCH, BUT IT KEPT ME OUT OF THE WAR FOR A YEAR."
—ABE

"EFFIE LOU IS A MAN! GET HIM! HE COULD THREATEN MY RECORD FOR LADY TRIPLES!"

AFTER ENTERING WORLD WAR II, HE LEADS
A COMBAT SQUAD KNOWN AS "THE FLYING HELLFISH"
AND LATER HAS A WRESTLING CAREER AS
"GLAMOROUS GODFREY, KING OF THE HEELS."

"YEP. I MAY JUST BE THE BEST KNOWN ABRAHAM IN HISTORY."

The Marriage of

Abraham Simpson
and Mona Olsen.

FOR IT IS ABE
AND MONA'S UNION
THAT RESULTS IN
ONE OF THE MOST
EARTHSHAKING
EVENTS OF
THE MODERN AGE...

The Birth
of
Homer Simpson

BECAUSE ALL BIG THINGS START OFF SMALL...

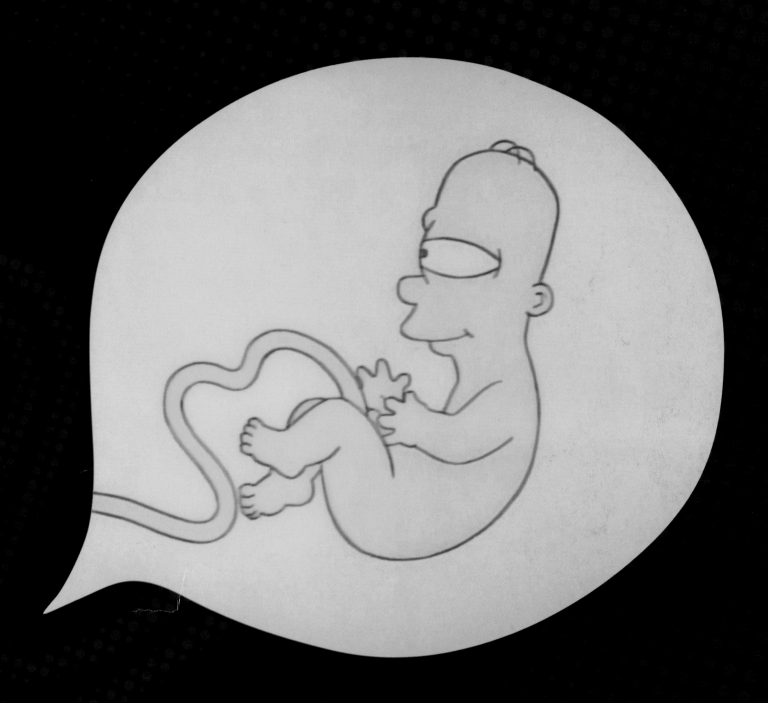

"WE'RE A TEAM!
AFTER ALL, IT'S 'UTER-US,' NOT 'UTER-YOU.'"
—HOMER

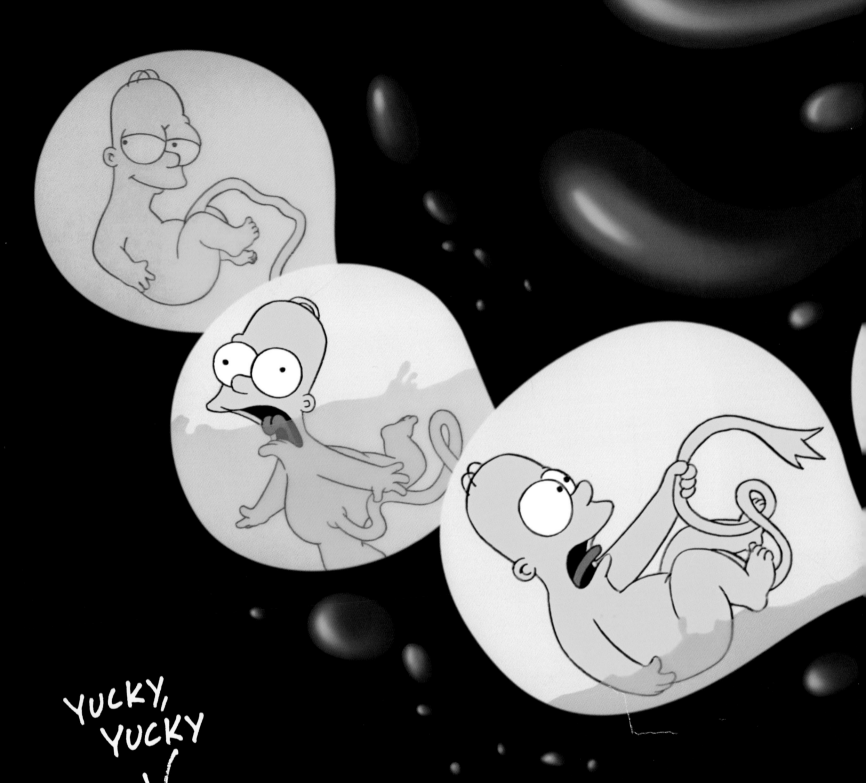

IT'S A BOY!

...THEN AGAIN,
LIFE IN THIS WORLD
AIN'T SO BAD.

AFTER ALL,
THERE'S PIZZA!

Springfield Shopper
DAILY NEWS   5¢

UNUSUALLY LARGE, UGLY BABY BORN

A COPY OF THE
"SPRINGFIELD SHOPPER"
THE DAY AFTER HOMER'S BIRTH.
SURPRISINGLY, THEY FORGOT TO PUT
THE DATE ON THE PAPER THAT DAY.

BABY ON BOARD

HOMER HAS TROUBLE ADJUSTING TO HIS NEW
SURROUNDINGS, AND NEITHER MONA
NOR ABE KNOW HOW TO COMFORT THEIR
NOT-SO-LITTLE BUNDLE OF JOY.

CANINE CANOODLE

WHEN BONGO THE FAMILY DOG
ENTERS, HE KNOWS JUST
WHAT TO DO.

"WHADDYA KNOW?
HE LIKES IT!"

THE MOMS THEY ARE A-CHANGIN'

AS HOMER GROWS, MOTHER AND SON ENJOY A HAPPY RELATIONSHIP...

♪ Ooey gooey rich and chewy inside

Golden flaky tender cakey outside... ♪

...BUT HER MARRIAGE TO ABE IS NOT WHAT MONA HOPED IT WOULD BE.

"WOULD YOU TWO PIPE DOWN? I'M TRYING TO WATCH THE SUPER BOWL. IF PEOPLE DON'T SUPPORT THIS THING, IT MIGHT NOT MAKE IT."

WHEN MONA CATCHES A GLIMPSE OF SUPERSTAR QUARTERBACK JOE NAMATH, HER WORLD IS TURNED UPSIDE DOWN.

"LOOK AT THEM SIDEBURNS. HE LOOKS LIKE A GIRL!"

—ABE

"HIS WILD, UNTAMED FACIAL HAIR REVEALED A NEW WORLD OF REBELLION, OF CHANGE. A WORLD WHERE DOORS WERE OPEN FOR WOMEN LIKE ME."

—MONA

RADICAL DUDES

MONA SOON FINDS LIKE-MINDED PEOPLE AT THE STATE COLLEGE. SHE STUMBLES UPON A RALLY OPPOSING THE GERM WARFARE LAB ON CAMPUS...

...A LABORATORY THAT'S OWNED BY C. MONTGOMERY BURNS, THE RICHEST MAN IN SPRINGFIELD.

GERM WARFARE LABORATORY
"When the H-Bomb Isn't Enough"

"HOW COULD I NOT BECOME A RADICAL WHEN WE WERE FIGHTING A FORCE OF PURE EVIL?"

—MONA

MY MOTHER THE ANARCHIST

WITH MONA'S GROWING
INTEREST IN ACTIVISM,
HOMER IS LEFT ALONE
MORE AND MORE OFTEN.

"SEE YOU LATER, HONEY.
MOMMY HAS TO GO CHAIN HERSELF
TO A NUCLEAR SUBMARINE.
HUGS AND KISSES!"

HE BECOMES STARVED FOR AFFECTION.

HE SEARCHES FOR SOMETHING TO FILL THE VOID
LEFT BY HIS ABSENT MOTHER.

AND WHEN HE FINDS IT, IT'S...

FINGER-LICKIN' GOOD!

WOODSTOCK OR BUST

HOPING TO SHARE HER NEW INTERESTS WITH HER FAMILY, MONA TAKES THEM TO A MUSIC FESTIVAL.

ABE FINDS IT INTOLERABLE...

BOWZER FOR PRESIDENT

"BOOO!
BRING ON
SHA NA NA!"
—ABE

...BUT HOMER HAS THE TIME OF HIS LIFE.

ABE SOON HAS ALL HE
CAN STOMACH AND
TAKES HIS SON HOME.

"LOOK AT ME!
I'M A HIPPIE!"

—HOMER

"SHAME ON YOU, BOY. PUT SOME DAMN PANTS ON
AND THEN PULL 'EM DOWN, 'CAUSE IT'S TIME FOR A SPANKING."

FREAK FLAG FLYIN'

SADDENED BY HER HUSBAND'S STUBBORNNESS, MONA PAINTS A MURAL FOR HOMER.

SHE HOPES IT WILL INSPIRE HIM TO LIVE LIFE FREE AND UNRESTRAINED.

SIMPSON FAMILY FUN FACT!

SIMPSON MEN ARE BORN CUTE AS A BUTTON!
(UNFORTUNATELY, THE SIMPSON GENES TAKE OVER AROUND AGE 3 AND ALL CUTENESS IS OBLITERATED BY AGE 4.)

HOMER, AGE 2:
AWWW...

HOMER, AGE 4:
YIKES!

BOMB SQUAD

MONA AND HER FELLOW RADICALS TAKE DRASTIC
ACTION TO SHUT DOWN MR. BURNS' GERM WARFARE LAB.

THEY CREATE A DEVICE THAT
RELEASES ANTIBIOTICS INTO
THE FACILITY AND DESTROYS
THE DEADLY VIRUSES.

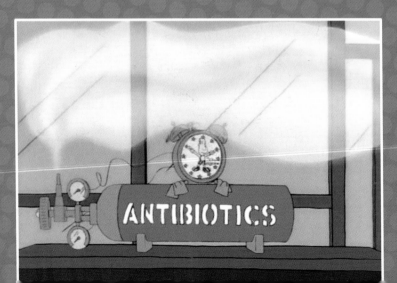

"MY GERMS! MY PRECIOUS GERMS!
THEY NEVER HARMED A SOUL! THEY
NEVER EVEN HAD THE CHANCE!"

MONTY ARRIVES AT THE LAB TO STOP THE CULPRITS...

"WHOEVER DID THIS WON'T GET PAST ME."

...BUT GETS TRAMPLED AS THE ACTIVISTS MAKE THEIR ESCAPE.

MONA RETURNS TO HELP THE FALLEN MR. BURNS.

"YOU POOR MAN. LET ME HELP YOU UP."

IT'S A DECISION SHE REGRETS INSTANTLY.

"YOU JUST MADE A VERY BIG MISTAKE. YOU'RE GOING TO SPEND THE REST OF YOUR LIFE IN PRISON WHEN I GET MY HANDS ON YOU!"

—MR. BURNS

MONA FLEES INTO THE NIGHT, REALIZING THAT LIFE AS SHE KNEW IT NO LONGER EXISTS.

SOON, MONA'S LIKENESS IS ALL OVER THE NATIONAL NEWS.

"ONLY ONE MEMBER OF THE SPRINGFIELD SEVEN WAS IDENTIFIED. SHE'S BEEN DESCRIBED AS A WOMAN IN HER EARLY THIRTIES, YELLOW COMPLEXION, AND MAY BE EXTREMELY HELPFUL."

CHOOSING BETWEEN HER SAFETY AND THAT OF HER LOVED ONES, MONA MAKES THE ULTIMATE SACRIFICE. SHE FORCES HERSELF TO LEAVE HER FAMILY IN HOPES OF SPARING THEM ANY FURTHER INVOLVEMENT.

GOODBYE, YELLOW THICK LAD

SHE STEALS INTO HOMER'S ROOM AND SAYS HER TENDER GOODBYES.

FOR HOMER, THAT KISS IS A WONDERFUL DREAM.

WANTED:

NAME UNKNOWN

MA'AM ON THE LAM

MONA PREPARES HERSELF FOR LIFE ON THE RUN.

SAYING GOODBYE TO HOMER IS THE HARDEST THING SHE HAS EVER DONE.

**SAYING GOODBYE TO ABE...
NOT SO MUCH.**

WITH MONA GONE,
ABE DOES HIS BEST
TO KEEP HIS SON
ENTERTAINED.

ND A BABY

"HEH, HEH. WANT MY KEYS, DO YA?"

HE SOON LEARNS THAT PARENTING ISN'T AS EASY AS HE FIRST BELIEVED.

"YAAAAY!"

"GET BACK HERE!"

HOMER'S ODYSSEY

GROWING UP WITHOUT A MOM AND RAISED BY A SURLY DAD SETS HOMER APART FROM THE OTHER KIDS IN THE NEIGHBORHOOD.

NO MATTER WHERE HE GOES, IT SEEMS LIKE HE'S JUST NOT WANTED.

NO HOMERS CLUB

HOMER MAKES THE BEST OF HIS LOT IN LIFE. IN TIME, HE FINDS A FEW GOOD FRIENDS AND SETTLES INTO A HAPPY PRETEEN ROUTINE.

HE EVEN GETS TO GO TO SUMMER CAMP...

CAMP SEE-A-TREE

FOR UNDERPRIVILEGED BOYS

...WHERE HE MEETS A MYSTERIOUS GIRL FROM A NEIGHBORING GIRLS' CAMP. HE NEVER LEARNS HER NAME, BUT THE TWO SHARE SOMETHING VERY SPECIAL.

First

"It was as satisfying as a million Hallmark cards with all the right-sized envelopes."

—MYSTERY GIRL

Kiss

"It felt like a cluster bomb wiping out a graveyard full of zombies."

—HOMER

FALLING FOR YOU

STILL DIZZY FROM THE EUPHORIA OF THAT KISS, HOMER MAKES A SINGLE MISSTEP (BUT IT'S A DOOZY!) WHILE WALKING THROUGH THE NIGHT WOODS.

HE'S SENT HOME AND NEVER GETS A CHANCE TO LEARN HIS SWEETHEART'S NAME.

SIMPSON FAMILY FUN FACT!

THE RECIPIENT OF HOMER'S FIRST KISS IS A YOUNG GIRL NAMED MARGE BOUVIER.

USUALLY SPORTING HAIR OF A SOFT BLUE HUE, HER BRUNETTE LOCKS WERE THE RESULT OF AN UNFORTUNATE IRONING MISHAP.

MORE ON HER LATER!

FAST TIMES AT SPRINGFIELD HIGH

AN UNEVENTFUL ADOLESCENCE EVENTUALLY
GIVES WAY TO THE TEENAGE YEARS AS HOMER BECOMES
A BORDERLINE-AVERAGE HIGH SCHOOL STUDENT.

HIS LIFE CENTERS AROUND MUSIC,
CARS, AND HIS BUDDIES.

♪ SOME PEOPLE CALL ME MAURICE! ♪ WOO WOOO!

MEET HOMER'S PALS!

CARL CARLSON
JAZZY!
SNAZZY!

LENNY LEONARD
FRIZZY!
WHIZZY!

BARNEY GUMBLE
BREEZY!
QUEASY!

HOMER BUYS HIS FIRST BEER

FEWER MOMENTS HAVE HAD A MORE PROFOUND EFFECT ON HOMER THAN THE PURCHASE (AND SUBSEQUENT PARTAKING) OF HIS VERY FIRST BEER. IT'S SAFE TO SAY THAT THE HOMER SIMPSON WE ALL KNOW WOULDN'T EXIST WITHOUT THE INFLUENCE OF ALL THAT DUFF BEER!

"ALCOHOL: THE ANSWER TO AND CAUSE OF ALL LIFE'S PROBLEMS!"

–HOMER

THE FABLED FAKE I.D.

WILL THE CLERK FALL FOR IT?

EH...SURE, WHY NOT?

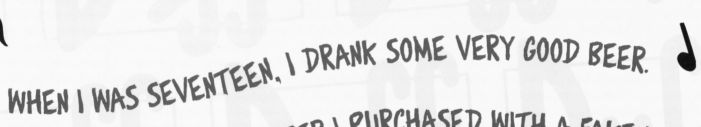 WHEN I WAS SEVENTEEN, I DRANK SOME VERY GOOD BEER.

I DRANK SOME VERY GOOD BEER I PURCHASED WITH A FAKE I.D.

 MY NAME WAS BRIAN McGEE.

I STAYED UP LISTENING TO QUEEN.

WHEN I WAS SEVENTEEN...

MARGE AT LARGE

LITTLE DOES HOMER SUSPECT THAT HE'LL ONCE AGAIN CROSS PATHS WITH THE MYSTERIOUS GIRL FROM HIS PAST. THEIR FIRST KISS LONG FADED INTO MEMORY, THE TWO TEENS HAVE NEVER BEEN IN CONTACT DURING THE THREE AND A HALF YEARS THEY'VE SPENT AT THE SAME SCHOOL.

THAT ALL CHANGES ONE FATEFUL DAY.

MARGE BOUVIER

AGE:
SEVENTEEN

STATUS:
HIGH SCHOOL SENIOR

TURN-ONS:
PAINTING, PHOTOGRAPHY, FORENSICS, GENERAL ORDERLINESS

TURN-OFFS:
SMOKING, PEOPLE WHO ARE FAKE, THE PHRASE "KEEP ON TRUCKIN'" (IT SOUNDS DIRTY)

CHILDHOOD DREAM:
TO BE THE FIRST FEMALE ASTRONAUT

TOO COOL FOR SCHOOL

HOMER AND BARNEY DECIDE TO SKIP SHOP CLASS AND SNEAK OFF.

"OH DEAR, IT SMELLS LIKE THE SHOP KIDS ARE SMOKING AGAIN."

"WE MAY BE LATE FOR WOOD SHOP, BUT WE'RE EARLY FOR LUNCH. LET'S GO GRAB A BURGER."

"BOY, YOU NEVER STOP EATIN', AND YOU NEVER GAIN A POUND!"

"IT'S MY METABOMOLISM. I GUESS I'M JUST NATURALLY THIN."

"WELL, WELL, WELL. IF IT ISN'T HOMER SIMPSON AND BARNEY GUMBLE. SPRINGFIELD'S ANSWER TO CHEECH AND CHONG."

BUSTED BY PRINCIPAL DONDELINGER, HOMER AND BARNEY ARE SENTENCED TO...

DETENTION
THREE O'CLOCK.
OLD BUILDING. ROOM 106.

SCHOOLGIRL POWER

"I'M FOR EQUAL RIGHTS, BUT DO WE REALLY NEED A WHOLE AMENDMENT?"

WHAT BEGINS AS TWO FRIENDS DISCUSSING THE ISSUES OF THE DAY...

"OH, MARGE. YOU REALLY HAVE TO READ THIS."

...TURNS INTO AN EPIPHANY FOR YOUNG MARGE BOUVIER.

BRIMMING WITH NEWFOUND KNOWLEDGE, MARGE HOLDS A LUNCHTIME RALLY SUPPORTING WOMEN'S RIGHTS...

"... AND IN ANOTHER ARTICLE, I FOUND OUT THAT TO HIRE PROFESSIONALS TO DO ALL THE JOBS OF A HOUSEWIFE, WHO INCIDENTALLY IS NOT MARRIED TO A HOUSE, WOULD COST FORTY-EIGHT THOUSAND DOLLARS A YEAR!"

...WHERE SHE DECIDES TO HEAT THINGS UP.

"THE FIRST STEP TO LIBERATION IS TO FREE OURSELVES FROM THESE MALE-IMPOSED SHACKLES!"

BURN, MARGIE! BURN!

THE BRA BURNING DOESN'T QUITE GO AS PLANNED, HOWEVER.

THE BLAZE IS FIERCE, BUT MERCIFULLY SHORT-LIVED.

"I DIDN'T THINK IT WOULD BURN SO FAST. I GUESS IT'S THE TISSUE PAPER INSIDE."

LIKE MANY ACTIVISTS, MARGE DRAWS THE IRE OF THE AUTHORITIES. IN THIS CASE, IT'S AN ANGRY HIGH SCHOOL PRINCIPAL.

PRINCIPAL DONDELINGER SENTENCES MARGE TO ONE DAY OF...

DETENTION
THREE O'CLOCK.
OLD BUILDING. ROOM 106.

WHEN WORLDS COLLIDE

IT'S JUST ANOTHER BORING AFTERNOON IN DETENTION, BUT WHEN MARGE WALKS IN, HOMER'S LIFE CHANGES FOREVER.

THE MYSTERY GIRL APPEARS.

"HEY, WHO'S THAT?!"

FOR HOMER,
IT'S LOVE AT
FIRST SIGHT.

A MATCH MADE IN DETENTION

**WHEN MARGE TAKES A SEAT NEXT TO HOMER,
HE CAN'T BELIEVE HIS EYES.**

GREAT GOOGLY MOOGLY!

EVEN BARNEY IS SMITTEN WITH THE NEW GIRL.

"HEY! WOULD YOU LIKE TO GO TO THE--?"

"SHE'S MINE!"

THE JAILBIRDS COMPARE STORIES.

"I'M A POLITICAL PRISONER."

"I'M HERE FOR BEING ME. EVERY DAY I SHOW UP, ACT LIKE ME, AND THEY SLAP ME IN HERE."

THE TEENAGE GENTLEMAN'S GUIDE TO LANDING THE

GIRL OF YOUR DREAMS

Just follow these handy steps…

1. DOES SHE KNOW YOU EXIST?

- ☐ **NO** (Don't just stand there. Introduce yourself, for Pete's sake!)
- ☑ **YES** (Congratulations! You're ready for step 2!)

2. DOES SHE CARE?

- ☐ **NO** (Game over, dude.)
- ☐ **YES** (Way to go!)
- ☑ **UNDECIDED** (You've got work to do. Good luck, Romeo!)

FATHER KNOWS WORST

"WHAT'S THE MATTER, BOY? YOU HAVEN'T SAID 'BOO' ALL NIGHT, AND USUALLY I HAVE TO WRESTLE THE BUCKET OUT OF YOUR GREASY MITTS."

"DAD, I'M IN LOVE."

TURNING TO HIS FATHER FOR SOME LOVE ADVICE, HOMER LEARNS ABE'S SECRETS TO A HAPPY LIFE.

"SON, YOU'VE GOT TO SET YOUR SIGHTS LOW."

ABRAHAM SIMPSON'S SUREFIRE GUIDE TO AVOIDING FAILURE

☐ DON'T OVERREACH.
☐ BUY A DENTED CAR.
☐ ASPIRE TO A DEAD-END JOB.
☐ PURSUE THE LESS ATTRACTIVE GIRL.

"OH, I BLAME MYSELF. WE SHOULD HAVE HAD THIS TALK A LONG TIME AGO."

"I NEED SOME GUIDANCE, COUNSELOR."
—HOMER

SINCE HIS DAD WAS NO HELP, HOMER PAYS A VISIT TO MR. MCINTYRE, THE HIGH SCHOOL GUIDANCE COUNSELOR, FOR TIPS ON HOW TO WIN MARGE'S HEART.

"WELL, THAT'S NOT EXACTLY THE TYPE OF GUIDANCE I GIVE."

"BUT I LIKE TO THINK I DO SOMETHING HELPFUL FOR EVERY STUDENT M THROUGH Z. MY ADVICE IS TO TRY TO SHARE A COMMON INTEREST AND SPEND, SPEND, SPEND."

WHILE THERE, HOMER PICKS UP A PAMPHLET FOR THE NUCLEAR POWER PLANT THAT WILL BE OPENING SOON.

MR. MCINTYRE URGES HIM TO CONSIDER IT FOR A CAREER, AS IT'S THE ONLY PLACE IN TOWN THAT WON'T REQUIRE A COLLEGE DEGREE.

"IMAGINE ME, IN A NUCLEAR PLANT..."

KA-BOOOM!

"HA-HA! FAT CHANCE!"

WITH THE INSIGHTS LEARNED FROM MR. McINTYRE, HOMER JOINS THE DEBATE TEAM IN ORDER TO GET CLOSER TO MARGE BOUVIER.

THERE HE MEETS ARTIE ZIFF, A DEBATE CHAMPION, INTELLECTUAL WHIZ KID, AND RIVAL FOR MARGE'S ATTENTION.

HOMER AND ARTIE ENGAGE IN A MOCK DEBATE...

"THE NATIONAL SPEED LIMIT SHOULD BE LOWERED TO FIFTY-FIVE MILES PER HOUR."

"*FIFTY-FIVE!* THAT'S RIDICULOUS! SURE, THEY'LL SAVE A FEW LIVES, BUT MILLIONS WILL BE LATE!"

...AND IT'S NOT LONG BEFORE THEY'RE AT EACH OTHER'S THROATS.

HOMER IS ASKED TO
OFFER A REBUTTAL...

...WHICH HE DOES WITH GREAT PLEASURE.

DESPITE HOMER'S BEST EFFORTS, MARGE CAUTIOUSLY KEEPS HER DISTANCE.

"HEL-LO! YOU MAY NOT REMEMBER ME. I'M HOMER SIMPSON. I MOONED FOR REBUTTAL. YOU WANT TO GO OUT WITH ME?"

"WELL, I DON'T THINK YOU'RE MY TYPE."

"THE PROBLEM IS, YOU DON'T KNOW ME. I HAVE REFERENCES. JUST ASK COACH FLANAGAN, AND ASK MR. SECKOFSKY AND BARNEY GUMBLE."

Should a young Marge Bouvier go on a date with Homer Simpson?
Why not do what any enterprising young woman would do and check...

HOMER'S REFERENCES
Let's see what they have to say!

COACH FLANAGAN
Track and Field

"Homer Simpson? Oh, yeah. Junior Varsity shot-putter. I think if he applies himself, trains real hard, hits the weights, he could go another foot."

MR. SECKOFSKY
Wood Shop Teacher

"I had him for four years. Solid 'C' student. Made a lamp last year!"

BARNEY GUMBLE
Partner in Crime

"He's all things to all men, and maybe to one lucky gal."

IN THE END, MARGE DECIDES TO TURN DOWN THE DATE WITH A LITANY OF EXCUSES.

"YOU SEEM LIKE A NICE ENOUGH GUY, BUT I REALLY DON'T HAVE THE TIME. THE CITY FORENSICS CHAMPIONSHIP IS COMING UP, AND I ALSO TUTOR FRENCH PART-TIME."

HOMER SENSES HIS OPENING...

"FRENCH, EH? JUST THE SUBJECT I'M HAVING TROUBLE WITH. WHAT A COINCIDENCE. CAN ANYONE BE TOOTED?"

AND WITH THAT SIMPLE REQUEST, A STUDY SESSION IS SET UP AT THE SIMPSON HOUSE.

THE BIG NIGHT

THIS MAY BE JUST A SIMPLE STUDY DATE, BUT TO HOMER,
IT'S AN OPPORTUNITY TO IMPRESS THE GIRL OF HIS DREAMS.

DOIN' THE 'DO...

WHOA!

LOST A FEW MORE
HAIRS TODAY...

THERE'S PLENTY MORE
WHERE THAT CAME FROM!

HOMER PUTS ON SOME
MAKE-OUT MUSIC TO
"SET THE MOOD" FOR
THE LOVELY MARGE.

DON'T BE A BABY, LADY.
JUST BE A LADY, BABY.

BEAUTY AND THE BEAST

WHEN MARGE ARRIVES, THE TWO QUICKLY BEGIN STUDYING. TO THEIR MUTUAL SURPRISE, HOMER ISN'T HALF BAD AT LEARNING FRENCH.

"I CAN'T BELIEVE IT, IT'S STICKING. YOU'RE TELLING ME NEW STUFF, AND MINUTES LATER IT'S STILL THERE! AND IT'S ALL THANKS TO YOU."

THEY EVEN MANAGE TO GET IN A LITTLE STUDY BREAK.

DO THE HUSTLE

MARGE FINALLY BEGINS TO WARM UP TO HOMER.

"YOU KNOW, HOMER, YOU'RE LIKE NO ONE I'VE EVER MET BEFORE. YOU'RE DEAR AND HONEST AND OPEN, WITHOUT A TRACE OF PRETENSION."

OOH LA LA!

EMBOLDENED BY MARGE'S COMPLIMENTS, HOMER ASKS HER TO THE PROM.

"MARGE, WOULD YOU GO TO THE PROM WITH ME?"

HER ANSWER IS A RESOUNDING "OUI."

FRENCH TO ENGLISH DICTIONARY

oui |wē|
exclam.
1. used to give an affirmative response
   • expressing agreement with a positive statement.
   • expressing contradiction of a negative statement.

WOO-HOO!

"THIS'LL BE THE GREATEST NIGHT OF YOUR LIFE. I'M RENTING THE BIGGEST LIMO. I'M GONNA BUY YOU THE BIGGEST CORSAGE. MY TUX IS GONNA HAVE THE WIDEST LAPELS, THE MOST RUFFLES, AND THE HIGHEST PLATFORM SHOES YOU EVER SAW!"

—HOMER

"I THINK I'LL WEAR MY HAIR...UP."

A FAUX PAS

MISREADING THE MOMENT, HOMER
MAKES A STARTLING CONFESSION.

"IF HONEST AND OPEN IS WHAT YOU
LIKE, GET A LOAD OF THIS. I'M NOT
REALLY IN ANY FRENCH CLASS. THIS
WAS JUST A BRILLIANT SCHEME TO
GET TO KNOW YOU BETTER."

SMACK!

MARGE
DOESN'T
HANDLE THE
NEWS VERY
WELL.

AFTER MARGE STORMS OUT, HOMER DOESN'T QUITE KNOW HOW TO REACT.

HE REFLECTS FOR A FEW MINUTES AND THEN SPRINGS INTO ACTION.

"HELLO, BARNEY? GUESS WHO'S GOT A DATE FOR THE PROM!"

THE NEXT DAY MARGE RUNS INTO ARTIE ZIFF AFTER THE CITY FORENSICS FINALS...

"MARGE, THIS MAY NOT BE THE MOST APPROPRIATE FORUM FOR WHAT I AM ABOUT TO PUT FORTH, BUT WOULD YOU GO TO THE PROM WITH ME?"

HAVING COMPLETELY FORGOTTEN ABOUT HOMER SIMPSON, MARGE ACCEPTS.

"ARTIE, I'VE KNOWN AND RESPECTED YOU FOR EIGHT YEARS. I WOULD BE DELIGHTED TO GO WITH YOU."

WILL HE BE A DREAM OR A DUD?

MARGE GETS READY FOR HER DATE, NOT REALIZING WHAT (OR WHO) AWAITS HER DOWNSTAIRS.

"If you pinch your cheeks, they'll glow. A little more. Try to break some capillaries, dear."

—MRS. BOUVIER

HOMER'S RECEPTION AT THE BOUVIER HOUSE IS LUKEWARM TO SAY THE LEAST.

"WHO OR WHAT ARE YOU?"

MISTAKING HOMER FOR SOMEONE ELSE, MARGE'S DAD CHIMES IN.

"YOU KNOW, I USUALLY INSIST ON APPROVING MARGE'S DATES, BUT FROM WHAT SHE'S TOLD ME I'M SURE YOU'RE A SOLID CITIZEN."

"THANKS, MR. B."

OF COURSE, IT NEVER OCCURS TO HOMER THAT HE DOESN'T BELONG THERE.

"HERE SHE COMES. GET THE CAMERA READY."

A Date with

Destiny

UNFORTUNATELY, MARGE WAS EXPECTING
SOMEONE ENTIRELY DIFFERENT.

WHAT ARE YOU DOING HERE?

"YOU SAID YOU'D GO TO THE PROM WITH ME."

"I ALSO SAID I HATED YOU, AND WE HAVEN'T EVEN TALKED SINCE THEN."

HOMER'S REASONING

"I WAS AFRAID YOU'D CANCEL OUR DATE SO I STAYED AWAY FROM YOU COMPLETELY, EVEN THOUGH IT MEANT SKIPPING SCHOOL FOR THREE WEEKS AND GRADUATING THIS SUMMER... I HOPE."

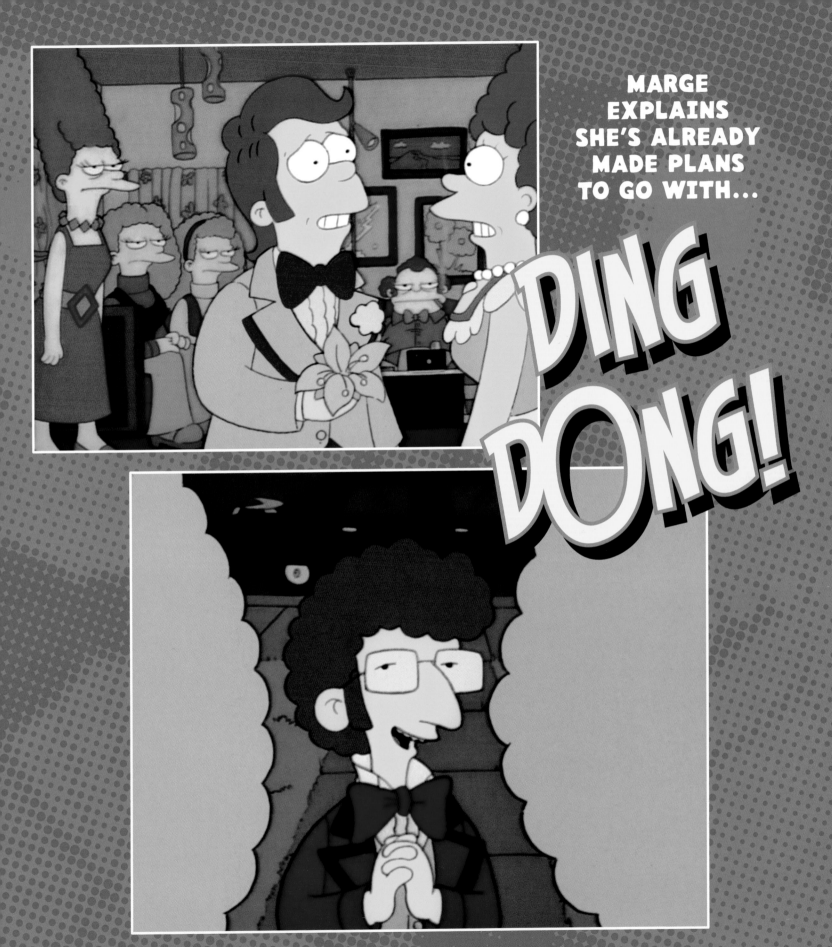

MARGE EXPLAINS SHE'S ALREADY MADE PLANS TO GO WITH...

DING DONG!

"HELLO, I'M ARTIE ZIFF, MARGE'S DATE FOR THE PROM."

A SUITOR SPURNED

FEELING LIKE A FIFTH WHEEL, HOMER RETREATS TO THE SOLITUDE OF HIS RENTED LIMOUSINE.

"Hey, buddy, where's your date?"

—CHAUFFEUR

"SHE'S WITH HIM."

WITH A HEAVY HEART, HOMER DECIDES TO MAKE THE BEST OF A SAD SITUATION.

"HEY, I PAID FOR THIS CAR, I PAID FOR THIS TUXEDO, AND I PAID FOR THE TWO DINNERS. I'M GOING TO THE PROM."

DESTINATION: PROM

n the Prom!
GOODBYE YELLOW BRICK ROAD
THE LARRY DAVIS EXPERIENCE
...AND NO STREAKING!

3 IS THE LONELIEST NUMBER

MARGE DOES HER BEST TO ENJOY PROM...

...BUT HOMER IS A LITTLE LESS SUCCESSFUL.

I present your senior class prom king and queen...

Artie Ziff and Marge Bouvier!

"INSTEAD OF VOTING FOR SOME ATHLETIC HERO, OR A PRETTY BOY, YOU HAVE ELECTED ME, YOUR INTELLECTUAL SUPERIOR, AS YOUR KING. GOOD FOR YOU!"

"ISN'T SHE GREAT? HAIL QUEEN MARGE! LONG LIVE THE QUEEN!"

THE ROYAL COUPLE SHARES A SPOTLIGHT DANCE...

Why do birds suddenly appear, Every time you are near...

...BUT IT'S TOO MUCH FOR THE HEARTBROKEN HOMER TO BEAR.

"I GOTTA GET OUTTA HERE."

"WHY ARE YOU DOING THIS, HOMER?"

"BECAUSE I'M SURE WE WERE MEANT TO BE TOGETHER. USUALLY WHEN I HAVE A THOUGHT, THERE'S A LOT OF OTHER THOUGHTS IN THERE. SOMETHING SAYS YES, SOMETHING SAYS NO. BUT THIS TIME THERE'S ONLY YES."

GETTING TO THE POINT

AFTER THE PROM, ARTIE TAKES MARGE TO SPRINGFIELD'S "INSPIRATION POINT," A POPULAR SPOT WITH THE LOCAL TEENS...

...WHERE IT TURNS OUT THE LECHEROUS MR. ZIFF IS NOT QUITE THE GENTLEMAN HE PRETENDS TO BE.

"ARTIE, I SAID STOP!"

MARGE SHOWS HIM THAT'S NO WAY TO TREAT A LADY.

SUH-LAP!

"TAKE ME HOME THIS INSTANT!"

"I WOULD APPRECIATE IT IF YOU DIDN'T TELL ANYBODY ABOUT MY 'BUSY HANDS.' NOT SO MUCH FOR MYSELF, BUT I AM SO RESPECTED IT WOULD DAMAGE THE TOWN TO HEAR IT."

-ARTIE ZIFF

HIS APOLOGY FALLS ON DEAF EARS.

TAKE THE LONG WAY HOME

"WELL, IT'S ONE O'CLOCK. IF YOU WANT TO KEEP ME, I'M AFRAID IT'S GONNA BE FORTY-FIVE DOLLARS AN HOUR."

BROKE AND ALONE, HOMER WALKS BACK HOME, HOPING TO CLEAR HIS HEAD.

HE DOESN'T EVEN NOTICE WHEN MARGE AND ARTIE DRIVE PAST.

IT'S AT THAT MOMENT THAT MARGE REALIZES JUST WHO SHE SHOULD HAVE GONE TO PROM WITH.

ON THE ROAD AGAIN

A FAMILIAR CAR SOON PULLS UP TO HOMER AND THE DRIVER OFFERS HIM A LIFT.

"MARGE? WHAT ARE YOU DOING HERE?"

"HI, PROM DATE. NEED A RIDE?"

FINALLY ALONE WITH HIS DREAM GIRL, HOMER USES HIS CORSAGE TO MEND MARGE'S TORN DRESS. MARGE BEAMS, KNOWING THAT SHE'S MADE THE RIGHT DECISION.

AN OAFISH SIR AND A GENTLEMAN

AFTER A ROMANTIC DRIVE BACK TO THE BOUVIER HOUSE, HOMER CONFESSES THAT HE'S GOING TO HUG AND KISS MARGE AND IS NEVER GOING TO LET HER GO.

And he seals that promise...

THE MANY FACES

THE OXY-MORON

THE STARTER 'STACHE

THE ATHLETIC SUPPORTER

FONZ-A-RIFFIC

OF TEEN HOMER

THE KABUKI ROCKER

CHIPPENDALE FAIL

THE HENPECKED HERO

THE FUTURE HUSBAND

INGENUES IN THE NEWS

MARGE AND FELLOW STUDENT CHLOE TALBOT ARE BOTH RISING STARS IN THE EXCITING WORLD OF HIGH SCHOOL JOURNALISM.

THEY BREAK THE BIGGEST NEWS STORY OF THE SEMESTER WHEN THEY DISCOVER THAT ONE OF THE CAFETERIA WORKERS IS SPITTING IN THE SOUP.

"THAT'LL TEACH YOU TO GIVE ME MY FIRST JOB OUT OF PRISON."

—MOE

FOR THEIR SCOOP, THEY ARE GIVEN THE HIGHEST AWARD THAT SPRINGFIELD HIGH HAS TO OFFER.

"LADIES, IT IS MY GREAT PLEASURE TO AWARD YOU THESE CERTIFICATES OF MERIT.
IN THIS BOX MARKED 'HONOREE,' FILL IN YOUR NAMES.
AND OVER HERE, WRITE IN WHAT YOU DID."

MARGIE'S CHOICE

AS GRADUATION APPROACHES, MARGE'S DREAM OF GOING OFF TO JOURNALISM SCHOOL IS PUT ASIDE IN ORDER TO BE NEAR HER SWEETHEART.

"STAY WITH ME, MARGE, AND I PROMISE WE'LL TRAVEL THE WORLD...AND PERHAPS OUTER SPACE."

COLLEGE BOUND VS. A HOUND

AS HIGH SCHOOL DRAWS TO A CLOSE,
HOMER MUST DECIDE WHAT PATH HE'LL TAKE.

"HOMER, JUST SIGN THIS APPLICATION, AND YOU'RE A SHOO-IN FOR COLLEGE."

"I DID ALWAYS WANT TO GO TO COLLEGE, BUT FATE STOOD IN THE WAY."

—HOMER

"LOOK AT THAT! THAT DOG HAS SOMEBODY'S HAM. THIS I GOTTA SEE!"

"GIMME THAT HAM, YOU STUPID DOG! GIMME!"

THE UNSIGNED APPLICATION ENDS UP IN THE "CIRCULAR FILE."

BONUS FUN FACT! HOMER NEVER GOT THE HAM, EITHER.

IT'S A HELL OF A TOWN

AFTER GRADUATION, HOMER TREATS HIMSELF TO A VACATION IN NEW YORK. HE'D ALWAYS BEEN FASCINATED BY THE BUSTLING CITY, BUT THE TRIP DOESN'T TURN OUT QUITE THE WAY HE IMAGINED.

FIRST, SOMEONE MAKES OFF WITH HIS CAMERA AS HE POSES FOR A PICTURE.

WHEN HE COMPLAINS TO A POLICE OFFICER, THE COP STEALS HIS LUGGAGE.

HE'S SLIGHTED BY THE RESIDENTS OF THE BIG APPLE AT EVERY TURN.

THUS BEGINS A LIFELONG AVERSION TO NEW YORK CITY.

"I GUESS I'M NOT IN SPRINGFIELD ANYMORE."

OH, AND THINGS REALLY GET BAD WHEN HE MEETS THE C.H.U.D.*

*Cannibalistic Humanoid Underground Dwellers

THE OPENING OF MOE'S BAR

SUCH A WONDERFUL NIGHT. THE FLOORS ARE STICKY WITH PROMISE.

"WELCOME TO MEAUX'S TAVERN. OR MOE'S TAVERN. WHATEVER."

SADLY, THE EVENING ISN'T A SUCCESS WITH MARGE, AS HOMER SPENDS THE ENTIRE NIGHT PLAYING VIDEO GAMES WITH HIS PALS.

SHE DOES GET TO FEED HIM NACHOS WHILE HE'S PLAYING, SO THERE'S THAT.

"VIDEO GAMES AND TOO MUCH BEER. YOU SURE KNOW HOW TO SHOW A GIRL A GOOD TIME."

BLEEAARR

"THE ONLY DANGEROUS AMOUNT OF ALCOHOL IS NONE!"

-HOMER

AT HER WIT'S END, MARGE PENS A BREAKUP NOTE TO HOMER AS HE'S BEING CARTED AWAY BY PARAMEDICS.

GH!

BUT AT THE HOSPITAL, SHE HAS A CHANGE OF HEART.

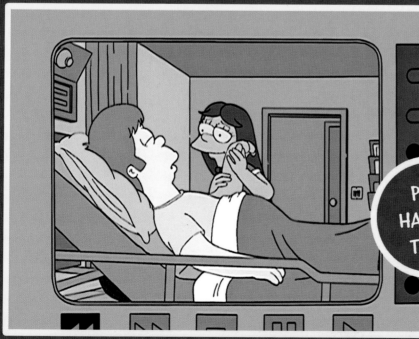

"WHATEVER PROBLEMS WE HAVE, WE HAVE A LIFETIME TO WORK THEM OUT...TOGETHER."

ROOMMATING FOR LIFE

HOMER AND MARGE SOON TAKE THE LEAP AND MOVE IN TOGETHER.

THEY DON'T HAVE A LOT OF MONEY, BUT THEY ARE YOUNG AND IN LOVE.

"WITH YOU, BABY, TOP RAMEN TASTES LIKE CUP O' NOODLES."

"YOU KNOW, THESE FOAM FUTONS DO VELCRO TOGETHER..."

"I'M SORRY, I'M NOT READY TO DO THAT YET. I WANT TO WAIT UNTIL I'M MARRIED...

...OR AT LEAST REALLY DRUNK."

THEY DECIDE TO FOLLOW THE EXAMPLE OF CURRENT CELEBRITY ROLE MODELS.

COLOR ME BLANDD

LIKE MANY YOUNG PEOPLE, HOMER HAS A MUSICAL DREAM. THE DREAM OF INOFFENSIVE URBAN-LITE HIP-HOP SMOOTH GROOVES. HE SPENDS HIS DAYS WITH HIS BAND, PERFECTING THEIR SOUND.

I'LL MAKE RUB TO YOU, SHOW RESPECT FOR YOU, HUG SO SAFE AND STRONG, BACK RUB ALL NIGHT LONG.

ROLL CALL

♪ Homer ♪

Lenny ♪

♪ Carl ♪

Lou the Cop ♪

MARGE GOT MAIL

WHEN MARGE RECEIVES AN ACCEPTANCE PACKET FOR SPRINGFIELD UNIVERSITY, HOMER FEELS BLINDSIDED. MARGE NEVER TOLD HIM SHE WAS GOING TO APPLY TO COLLEGE.

"THAT'S NOT TRUE. I DID TELL YOU."

"I THOUGHT YOU WERE TELLING ME YOU WANTED TO APPLY YOURSELF TO MAKING A COLLAGE!

AS I RECALL, I WAS AGAINST IT."

—HOMER

MARGE WORRIES THAT HER DREAM MAY BE TOO EXPENSIVE TO COME TRUE. SEEING HOW MUCH THIS MEANS TO HER, HOMER VOWS TO PAY HER TUITION...AT GREAT PERSONAL SACRIFICE.

"BABY, YOU DESERVE EVERY LAST BIT OF IT. I CAN GET THE MONEY, BUT IT'LL MEAN SWALLOWING MY PRIDE AND WORKING FOR MY DAD."

TAG TEAM

IN ORDER TO MAKE GOOD ON HIS PROMISE, HOMER GOES TO WORK FOR HIS FATHER.

HOMER FINDS HIS NEW JOB INCREDIBLY TEDIOUS...

...AND THOSE ARE THE GOOD MOMENTS.

"THIS COUNTS AS YOUR BREAK."

COLLEGE GIRL

MARGE'S FIRST DAY AT SPRINGFIELD UNIVERSITY IS FILLED WITH WONDER AND DISCOVERY.

"SO BEAUTIFUL! THIS PLACE IS JUST LIKE THE BROCHURE."

"AUTUMN LEAVES"

"BULL SESSIONS"

"FRATERNITY PLEDGES IN THEIR BEANIES."

AND WHEN SHE ATTENDS HER FIRST CULTURAL HISTORY CLASS, MARGE MAKES THE MOST WONDERFUL DISCOVERY OF ALL...

Professor Stefane August

"OOH, I THINK I'M GOING TO LIKE IT HERE."

GROWING PAINS

HOMER VISITS MARGE ON CAMPUS, AND SHE TELLS HIM ABOUT ALL THE NEW FEELINGS COLLEGE HAS AWAKENED INSIDE HER.

"MY MIND HAS BEEN OPENED IN SO MANY WAYS. DID YOU KNOW EVERY U.S. PRESIDENT WAS A STRAIGHT WHITE MAN?"

"EVEN WALT DISNEY?"

AND WHEN SHE GUSHES ABOUT PROFESSOR AUGUST, HOMER JUST LAUGHS.

"WHO'S HE? SOME GRAY-HAIRED BOOKWORM?"

—HOMER

"NOT EXACTLY."

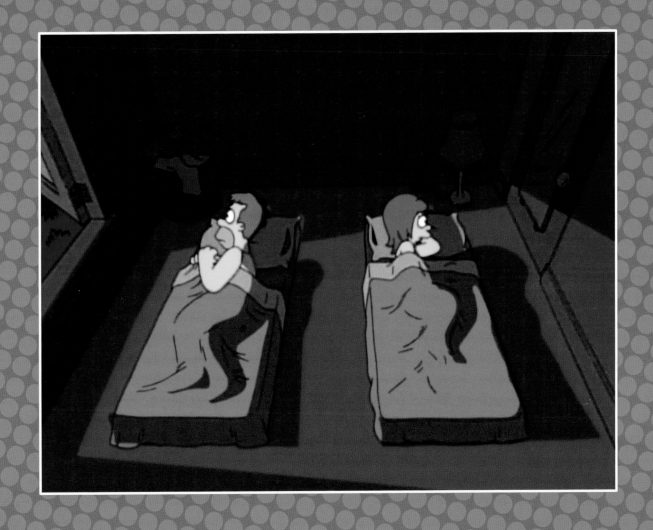

AS THE DAYS
GO BY, A DISTANCE
CREEPS INTO THE
ONCE HAPPY
COUPLE'S LIVES.
THEY SEEM TO
BE GROWING
IN DIFFERENT
DIRECTIONS, AND
NEITHER KNOWS
WHAT TO DO.

ONE NEW DIRECTION

WITH HIS PERSONAL LIFE IN DISARRAY, HOMER MAKES A CHANGE.

"OUR HARMONY-LADEN R&B DOESN'T MAKE SENSE IN THIS CRUEL WORLD. I'M TAKING OUR MUSIC TO THE NEXT LEVEL."

INTRODUCING **G.R.U.N.G.E**

GUITAR   ROCK   UTILIZING   NIHILIST   GRUNGE   ENERGY

HE CHANNELS ALL HIS FRUSTRATION INTO HIS MUSIC.

"WE ARE SADGASM, AND THIS SONG IS CALLED 'POLITICALLY INCORRECT.'"

♪ PAIN IS BROWN, HATE IS WHITE ♪ ♪
LOVE IS BLACK, STAB THE NIGHT ♪
♪ KINGDOM OF NUMB, CLOSET OF HURT ♪

FEELINGS ARE DUMB, KISSES ARE DIRT!

MARGE IS SHOCKED THAT HOMER'S MUSIC IS SO ANGRY AND BITTER.

"NOW WHY WOULD I BE ANGRY AND BITTER? BECAUSE I'M PAYING FOR YOU TO MAKE GOO-GOO EYES AT SOME SMOOTH-TALKING PROFESSOR?"

–HOMER

THE BREAKUP

WITH EMOTIONS RUNNING HOT,
MARGE AND HOMER HAVE THEIR FIRST FIGHT.

"HERE'S A QUESTION FOR YOU: WHY SHOULD I STAY WITH A MAN WHO RESENTS HOW I FLOWER?"

SARCASTIC VOICE

"WELL, IF YOU FEEL THAT WAY, MAYBE YOU CAN FIND SOMEONE WHO WANTS TO NURTURE THE NEW YOU. MAYBE A SOMEONE A LITTLE OLDER AND MORE SOPHISTICATED WHO CAN TAKE YOU TO EUROPE FOR THE SUMMER."

—HOMER

"FINE BY ME."

AND WITH THAT, MARGE AND STEFANE RIDE OFF TOGETHER.

STRIFE GOES ON

♪ RAZOR BLADE OF APATHY SHAVE ME WITH YOUR IRONY. SHAVE ME! SHAVE ME! SHAVE ME!!! ♪

SADGASM'S POPULARITY SOARS, FUELED BY HOMER'S ANGST-RIDDEN SONGS...

...WHILE MARGE COZIES UP TO HER CHARMING PROFESSOR.

"I WANT YOUR KNOWLEDGE INSIDE ME."

—MARGE

"MARGE, MAY I KISS YOUR MOUTH WITH MY MOUTH?"

—PROF. AUGUST

STEFANE BEGINS ROMANCING HIS LOVE-STRUCK STUDENT.

MARGIE and the PROFESSOR

BUT IT ISN'T LONG BEFORE MARGE GROWS TIRED OF STEFANE'S PRETENTIOUS WAYS. WHEN SHE CONFIDES IN HIM THAT SHE HOPES TO FIND A HUSBAND ONE DAY...

"MARGE, IT'S STATEMENTS LIKE THAT THAT MAKE PEOPLE SAY WOMEN ARE STUPID. I DON'T WANT TO SOUND MEAN. I'M JUST TRYING TO HELP YOU EVOLVE."

...STEFANE'S SMUG PSEUDO-PHILOSOPHY TAKES MARGE TO HER BREAKING POINT.

"EVOLVE YOURSELF, PROFESSOR JERK! OR SHOULD I SAY ASSOCIATE PROFESSOR JERK!"

HOMER ALONE

MEANWHILE, HOMER ACHIEVES EVERY ROCK STAR'S DREAM: HATING BEING FAMOUS. HE SPENDS HIS DAYS LOCKED IN A ROOM, DEVOURING PIZZA AND BLENDED COFFEE BEVERAGES.

"I'M THE HOTTEST GRUNGE ARTIST ON MUCOUS RECORDS. WHY AREN'T I HAPPY?"

TO COPE WITH THE PAIN, HE WRITES A SONG FOR HIS LOST LOVE AND TITLES IT "MARGERINE."

♪ ♪ spread yellow gunk on my pancake heart,

♪ I paid for her dreams, she taught me to cry.

I can't believe you're not mine!

Country churned girl in my grocery cart.

Like watery knives, like rain from my eyes.

margerine! Margerine!! MARGERINE!!!

"HE LOVES ME SO MUCH,
EVEN AFTER WHAT I DID TO HIM."

EALIZATION IS CUT
BY A NEWS FLASH.

TRAILBLAZERS **SADGASM**
EN UP. RECLUSIVE FRONTMAN,
MPSON, HAS HOLED HIMSELF
HIS MANSION AS RUMORS
BOUT AN OUT-OF-CONTROL
COTICS ADDICTION."

TO THE RESCUE

MARGE RUNS TO HOMER AND SEPARATES HIM FROM HIS DRUGS. SHE TAKES CARE OF HIM...

...BUT HE DOESN'T GET ANY BETTER.

LATER, MARGE LEARNS THE DRUG SHE TOOK FROM HOMER WAS INSULIN, NOT HEROIN.

"I HAD BECOME DIABETIC FROM DRINKING TOO MANY FRAPPUCCINOS."

—HOMER

MARGE ASKS HOMER'S FORGIVENESS...

"I GOT SO CAUGHT UP IN THE WORLD OF COLLEGE THAT I FORGOT HOW IMPORTANT YOUR LOVE WAS. CAN YOU FIND IT IN YOUR HEART TO TAKE ME BACK?"

THEY BECOME A HAPPY COUPLE ONCE AGAIN.

TWISTED SISTERS

WITH THEIR RELATIONSHIP BACK ON TRACK, HOMER AND MARGE BEGIN THE TASK OF REBUILDING THEIR FINANCES.

TO SAVE MONEY, MARGE MOVES BACK IN WITH HER FAMILY.

"I DON'T KNOW WHAT YOU SEE IN THAT UGLY MEATBALL. IF YOU LIKE BEING PAWED BY SOMETHING FAT AND LAZY, YOU SHOULD GET A CAT. IT'D LEAVE LESS HAIR ON THE COUCH."

BACHELOR PAD

HOMER CRASHES WITH HIS PAL BARNEY...

"WHAT'S ON THE TUBE?"

...WHERE THE TWO FRIENDS SPEND THEIR DAYS IN NOBLE PURSUITS.

"OH NO! I'VE LOST MY BIKINI TOP IN THE RIPTIDE!"

AWOO!

HUBBA! HUBBA!

Wednesday 4PM 5PM

6 Harley's Angels—Drama/Titillation 1:00
It's Aloha-time as the angels break out their hula skirts in order to solve a murder on the island of Hawaii.

Grits A Flyin'—Comedy 2:00
group of teenage misfits join

BACK TO THE GRIND

WITH ALL OF HOMER'S SADGASM EARNINGS
USED TO PAY FOR HIS HOSPITAL STAY, EACH MEMBER
OF THE YOUNG COUPLE TAKES A JOB AT ONE OF
SPRINGFIELD'S PREMIER HOT SPOTS.

FOR MARGE, WORKING AS A CARHOP
AT BERGER'S BURGERS BRINGS IN A LITTLE CASH.

AND HOMER BECOMES INVOLVED IN THE THRILL-A-MINUTE WORLD OF MINIATURE GOLF.

"HOMER, YOU'RE TURNING THE BLADES TOO FAST. THE GOLFERS ARE COMPLAINING. SLOW DOWN!"

HE'S EVEN ON THE MANAGEMENT FAST TRACK.

"KEEP UP THE GOOD WORK AND SOMEDAY YOU'LL BE THE GUY WHO HANDS OUT THE PUTTERS."

MARGE AND HOMER FALL INTO A HAPPY DATING ROUTINE.

MOVIES

SWEET TALK

"MARGE, YOU'RE AS PRETTY AS PRINCESS LEIA AND AS SMART AS YODA."

ADMIT ONE

AZTEC THEATER

SPACE MUTANTS IV: THE TRILOGY CONTINUES

SPACE MUTANTS IV: THE TRILOGY CONTINUES

ADMIT ONE

ROMANTIC DRIVES

...YOU LIGHT UP MY LIFE...

TO SIR PUTT-A-LOT'S, WITH LOVE

BUT ONE NIGHT, THE LOVEBIRDS FIND THEMSELVES HIDDEN AWAY INSIDE THE CASTLE OBSTACLE AT THE MINI GOLF COURSE...

"HONEY, SOMEDAY I'LL BUY YOU A REAL CASTLE."

IT TURNS OUT THE MINI
GOLFERS AREN'T THE ONLY
ONES GETTING LUCKY
THAT NIGHT.

Greetings FROM *SIR PUTT-A-LOT'S* MERRIE OLDE FUN CENTRE

FREE GAME WITH EVERY HOLE IN ONE!

M.B. PHONE HOMER

BARNACLE BILL'S
JUST ADD URINE!

HOME PREGNANCY TEST

IN THE WEEKS THAT FOLLOW, MARGE BEGINS TO NOTICE CERTAIN, SHALL WE SAY, "CHANGES."

"I'VE GOT A LOT OF NAUSEA AND AN UNEXPLAINED CRAVING FOR PANCAKE MIX."

—MARGE

SHE MAKES A CALL TO HOMER AND EXPLAINS THE DELICATE SITUATION.

"I NEED YOU TO DRIVE ME TO THE DOCTOR. REMEMBER THAT UNFORGETTABLE NIGHT WE...'JOINED THE CASTLE CLUB'?"

AT FIRST, HOMER IS OBLIVIOUS.

"OF COURSE, I DO. WHAT'S THE PROBLE--?"

HE EVENTUALLY CATCHES ON.

"OH."

BABY ON BOARD

AFTER EXAMINING MARGE,
DR. HIBBERT DELIVERS SOME UNEXPECTED NEWS.

"WELL, MS. BOUVIER, I THINK WE FOUND THE REASON YOU'VE BEEN THROWING UP IN THE MORNING. CONGRATULATIONS."

D'OH!

"OH DEAR."

HE EVEN PROVIDES A HELPFUL PAMPHLET.

SO YOU'VE RUINED YOUR LIFE

"YOU LUCKY BUM! THE FISH JUMPED RIGHT IN THE BOAT, AND ALL YOU'VE GOT TO DO IS WHACK HER WITH THE OAR!"

IT'S SURPRISINGLY SOUND ADVICE.

A HALFWAY DECENT PROPOSAL

HOMER TAKES MARGE UP TO THE OVERLOOK TO SHOW HER THE LIGHTS OF SPRINGFIELD. THE GENTLE GLOW FROM THE NUCLEAR PLANT'S COOLING TOWERS REALLY ADDS TO THE AMBIENCE.

THERE'S A QUESTION HE NEEDS TO ASK HER, BUT HE'S AFRAID. HE WORRIES THAT IF SHE SAYS NO, IT WILL DESTROY HIM.

"WELL, I HAVEN'T SAID NO TO YOU LATELY, HAVE I?"

—MARGE

"NUTS! I WROTE DOWN WHAT I WAS GOING TO SAY ON A CARD. THE STUPID THING MUST HAVE FALLEN OUT OF MY POCKET."

"IS THIS IT?"

"I DUNNO. WHAT'S IT SAY?"

GETTING TO YES

AS MARGE READS WHAT HOMER HAS WRITTEN, SHE BECOMES ENCHANTED BY HIS SWEETNESS.

FROM THE FIRST MOMENT I SAW YOU I NEVER WANTED TO BE WITH ANYONE ELSE. I DON'T HAVE MUCH TO OFFER YOU, EXCEPT ALL MY LOVE.

WILL YOU MARRY ME?

DESPITE HOMER'S DANGLING RUMP, MARGE IS OVERJOYED.

"OH, HOMER, THIS IS THE MOST BEAUTIFUL MOMENT OF MY LIFE."

"YES, I'LL MARRY YOU."

—MARGE

"WOO-HOO! SHE'S GONNA MARRY ME! IN YOUR FACE, EVERYBODY!"

—HOMER

LARD OF THE RINGS

NEWLY ENGAGED, HOMER AND MARGE MAKE THEIR WAY TO SPRINGFIELD'S PREMIER JEWELRY STORE...

...WHERE THE HAPPY COUPLE SHOPS FOR AN ENGAGEMENT RING.

SHORT ON CASH, BUT LONG ON AMBITION, HOMER SPOTS THE PERFECT SPECIMEN.

"WOW! I'LL TAKE THAT ONE."
—HOMER

"YES, SIR. AND HOW WILL YOU BE PAYING FOR IT?"

"I DON'T KNOW."

GOIN' TO THE CHAPEL

HOMER AND MARGE DRIVE TO A QUAINT LITTLE CHAPEL JUST ACROSS STATE LINES.

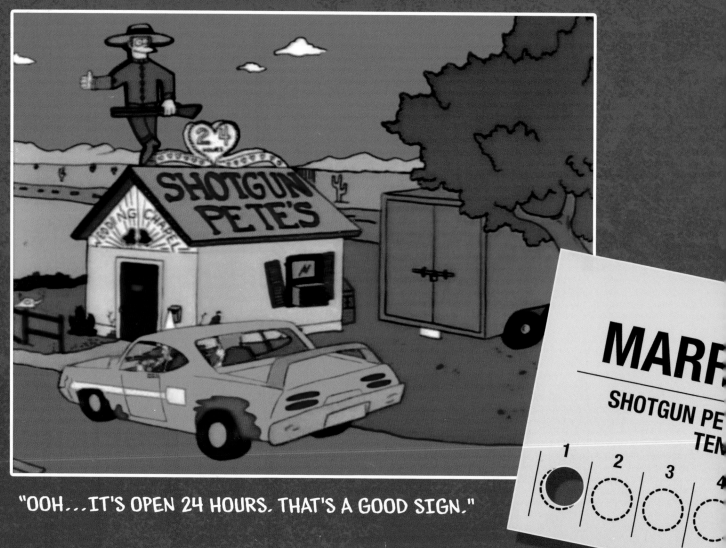

"OOH...IT'S OPEN 24 HOURS. THAT'S A GOOD SIGN."

"BASIC CEREMONY IS TWENTY BUCKS. HERE'S YOUR LICENSE. BE SURE TO GET THIS PUNCHED EVERY TIME."

"THE TENTH MARRIAGE IS ON THE HOUSE."

OFFICIAL
GE LICENSE
LOYALTY REWARDS CARD
ARRIAGE FREE
6   7   8   9   FREE

GIFT OF THE ABE GUY

AT THE WEDDING, ABE GIVES THE YOUNG COUPLE
A GENEROUS GIFT TO START THEIR LIFE TOGETHER.

"HERE YOU GO, HOMER.
IT MAY NOT BE MUCH,
BUT IT'S ALL I HAVE."

"GEE, THANKS, DAD."

SCREE!

THE LOCAL WILDLIFE HAS A DIFFERENT AGENDA, HOWEVER.

SCREE!

"AW, NUTS."

the HONEYMOONERS

AFTER THE CEREMONY, THE HAPPY NEWLYWEDS TAKE IN THE VIEW...

...OF A BILLBOARD NEXT TO THE SPRINGFIELD DUMP.

NOTHING SAYS "JUST MARRIED" LIKE THROWING UP IN A BUCKET.

BAD RECEPTION

HOMER FEELS TERRIBLE ABOUT THEIR LESS-THAN-ROMANTIC WEDDING. HE TRIES TO MAKE IT UP TO MARGE BY TAKING HER TO A DINER JUST OFF THE INTERSTATE.

"SEE? YOU DON'T HAVE TO SPEND A LOT OF MONEY TO HAVE A FIRST-CLASS RECEPTION."

To a Whale of a Wife

HIS CHOICE IN CAKES LEAVES SOMETHING TO BE DESIRED, BUT MARGE DOESN'T SEEM TO MIND.

SIMPSON FAMILY FUN FACT!

MARGE AND HOMER DID HAVE MORE HONEYMOON ADVENTURES, BUT INFORMATION IS SKETCHY AS DETAILS OF THE EVENT HAVE BEEN SEALED DUE TO A GAG ORDER. ALL THAT REMAINS IS THIS FAMILY PHOTO.

COURT DOCUMENTS REVEAL THE SETTLEMENT FOR DAMAGES WAS $68,000.

THE DAY ENDS WITH THE NEWLYWEDS RETURNING
HOME FOR THEIR FIRST NIGHT TOGETHER.

"WHAT A
PERFECT DAY."
—MARGE

"OUR FIRST NIGHT
TOGETHER AS MAN
AND WIFE."
—HOMER

"HEY, LOVEBIRDS.
KEEP IT DOWN
IN THERE!"
—PATTY

THEY SOON REALIZE THAT
LIVING WITH MARGE'S
FAMILY HAS ITS DRAWBACKS.

SO THAT EXPLAINS IT...

WHILE ATTENDING A SHIP CHRISTENING IN SPRINGFIELD HARBOR, A PREGNANT MARGE UNINTENTIONALLY DRINKS A DROP OF CHAMPAGNE...

"I NOW CHRISTEN THIS SHIP THE U.S.S. FLOAT-AND-SHOOT!"

...WHICH SETS HER UNBORN BABY UP FOR A LIFETIME OF DEVILISHNESS.

SONOGRAM SUCKERS

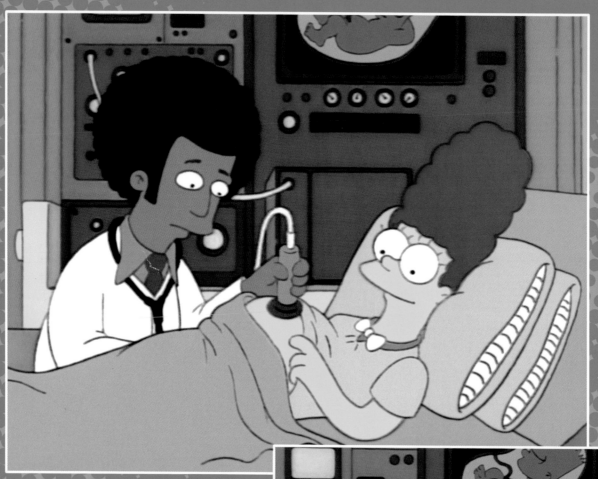

AS PART OF MARGE'S PRENATAL CARE, DR. HIBBERT USES THE LATEST TECHNOLOGY TO TAKE A PICTURE OF THE BABY.

"HMMMM..."

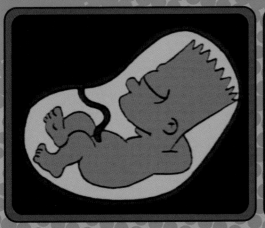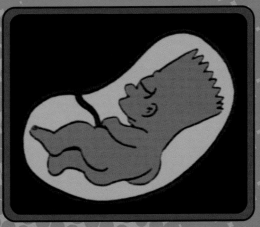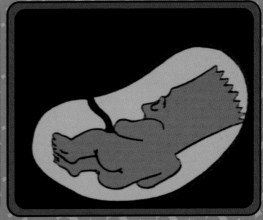

THE FETUS STRIKES A CHEEKY POSE
FOR THE YOUNG PHYSICIAN.

"IF I DIDN'T KNOW BETTER, I'D SWEAR HE WAS TRYING TO MOON US."

BABY BLING

HOMER GOES OVERBOARD
AND FILLS THE NURSERY
WITH EVERYTHING
THE NEW BABY COULD
POSSIBLY NEED.

WHEN MARGE
CALCULATES THE
COST, SHE SEES THAT
THINGS SIMPLY AREN'T
ADDING UP.

"HOMER, I DON'T SEE HOW WE CAN AFFORD ALL THESE THINGS ON YOUR SALARY."

"WHY DON'T YOU APPLY OVER AT THE NUCLEAR POWER PLANT?
I HEAR THEY PAY PRETTY WELL."

HOMER PROMISES TO GO AND INTERVIEW AT THE PLANT THE VERY NEXT DAY.

AT THE PLANT, THE INTERVIEW DOESN'T GO SO WELL.

APPLICANT EVALUATION

QUESTION 1: WHAT WOULD YOU SAY IS YOUR WORST QUALITY?

"WELL, I AM A WORKAHOLIC."

"I PUSH MYSELF TOO HARD."

"IT TAKES ME A LONG TIME TO LEARN ANYTHING, I'M KIND OF A GOOF-OFF, LITTLE STUFF STARTS DISAPPEARING FROM THE WORKPLACE..."

A DEFEATED HOMER
RETURNS TO THE
BOUVIER HOUSE AND
SHARES THE BAD
NEWS.

"I DIDN'T GET THE JOB.
THEY WANTED SOMEONE
GOOD. STORY OF MY LIFE."

HE MAKES A VOW
TO HIS UNBORN SON.

"KID, I SWEAR TO
YOU...WHEN YOU COME OUT
OF THERE, THE FIRST THING
YOU'RE GOING TO SEE IS A
MAN WITH A GOOD JOB."

"YEAH, THE
DOCTOR."

-PATTY

YE OLDE CANDLEMAKER SHOPPE

IN THE FOLLOWING WEEKS, HOMER TRIES HIS HAND AT MANY DIFFERENT JOBS.

FIRST IN OLDE SPRINGFIELD TOWNE, AT A TOURIST ATTRACTION WHERE HE INADVERTENTLY MAKES THE CHILDREN CRY.

"WHAT A CRAPPY CANDLE. YOU'VE RUINED MY VACATION."

HE'S QUICKLY FIRED BUT NOT BEFORE THE CHILDREN GET THEIR REVENGE.

THINGS AT THE DOG SCHOOL GO ABOUT AS WELL AS YOU'D EXPECT.

"I QUIT! I QUIT!"

–HOMER

"I THOUGHT YOU SAID YOU LIKED DOGS."

"...AND THE LADY'S RING, I'M AFRAID."

MARGE IS DEVASTATED, BUT SHE SURRENDERS HER RING.

"REPOSSESSING STUFF IS THE HARDEST PART OF MY JOB."

-REPO DEPOT EMPLOYEE #21355

HOMER ALONE

THAT NIGHT, HOMER WRITES A LETTER TO MARGE, ADMITTING HIS DEFEAT. HE PROMISES TO SEND HER EVERY CENT HE MAKES BUT WON'T RETURN UNTIL HE CAN SUPPORT HER AND THE BABY.

HE LEAVES THE NOTE BY HER BEDSIDE...

...AND DISAPPEARS INTO THE NIGHT.

FROM THE PEN OF

~~PATTY~~

HOMER

DEAR MARGE,

BY THE TIME YOU READ THIS I WILL BE GONE. YOU DESERVE ALL THE FINEST THINGS IN THE WORLD. AND ALTHOUGH I CAN GIVE THEM TO YOU, THEY WILL BE REPOSSESSED AND I WILL BE HUNTED DOWN LIKE A DOG. ALSO, IT HAS BECOME CLEAR THAT YOUR FAMILY DOESN'T WANT ME HERE. I WILL SEND YOU EVERY CENT I EARN FOR THE BABY, BUT YOU WILL NOT SEE ME AGAIN UNTIL I AM A MAN.

LOVE,
HOMER

MARGE IS CRUSHED WHEN SHE READS THE LETTER.

"THERE, THERE...WE'RE ALL IN SHOCK. I THOUGHT HE'D AT LEAST TWO-TIME YOU FIRST."
-PATTY

SECRET SAUCE

PATTY AND SELMA MAKE A STARTLING DISCOVERY AT THE LOCAL GULP 'N' BLOW.

BLECCH!

"THIS TACO IS FULL OF HAIR!"

"THERE'S YOUR EXPLANATION."

–SELMA

THEY FIND HOMER WORKING AS A LOWLY FAST-FOOD TRAINEE.

HE DOESN'T QUITE GET THE WHOLE "FOOD SAFETY" THING YET.

MAN OF HIS WORD

DEAR MARGE
× × ×
HOMER

IN THE WEEKS THAT FOLLOW, MARGE REGULARLY RECEIVES LETTERS FROM HOMER. HE DOESN'T SAY WHERE HE IS OR WHAT HE'S DOING, BUT ALL THE MONEY HE'S EARNED IS INCLUDED.

EVERY NIGHT, MARGE ANXIOUSLY AWAITS THE DAY HOMER WILL RETURN TO HER.

SEEING MARGE SO LONELY, SELMA SPILLS THE PROVERBIAL PINTO BEANS.

SHE TELLS HER SISTER THE TWO AND A HALF WORDS THAT LEAD MARGE TO HOMER...

"GULP 'N' BLOW."

DEVOTED AT THE DRIVE-THRU

TIME DRAGS AT WORK UNTIL HOMER RECEIVES A VERY SPECIAL VISITOR.

"YEAH, WHADDYA WANT?"

"MY HUSBAND BY MY SIDE."

WHEN HOMER REALIZES MARGE HAS COME TO SEE HIM, HE'S OVERJOYED.

AFTER
WEEKS OF
SEPARATION...

...HOMER
KNOWS JUST
WHAT TO SAY.

"HOLY COW! YOU'RE AS BIG AS A HOUSE!"

...AND USES ONE IN A ROMANTIC GESTURE.

"MARGE, POUR VOUS."
—HOMER

AND WITH THAT SIMPLE ACT, ALL IS SET RIGHT IN THEIR WORLD.

"WOULD YOU MIND IF I TOOK IT OFF NOW? THE OIL IS BURNING MY FINGER."

WELL-FED MAN WALKING

EMBOLDENED BY HIS MEETING WITH MARGE, HOMER MARCHES TO THE POWER PLANT TO DEMAND A JOB.

HE LETS NOTHING GET IN HIS WAY.

STORMING INTO THE OWNER'S OFFICE, HE PRESENTS ALL THE REASONS HE'D MAKE A GREAT EMPLOYEE.

"LISTEN TO ME, MR. BIG SHOT. IF YOU'RE LOOKING FOR THE KIND OF EMPLOYEE WHO TAKES ABUSE AND NEVER STICKS UP FOR HIMSELF, I'M YOUR MAN! YOU CAN TREAT ME LIKE DIRT, AND I'LL STILL KISS YOUR BUTT AND CALL IT ICE CREAM. AND IF YOU DON'T LIKE IT, I CAN CHANGE!"

INTERVIEW WITH A VAMPIRE

MR. BURNS LIKES WHAT HE SEES IN YOUNG HOMER AND HIRES HIM STRAIGHTAWAY.

"I LIKE YOUR ATTITUDE.
FEISTY, YET SPINELESS.
WELCOME ABOARD, SON."

-MR. BURNS

"I GOT THE JOB! I GOT THE JOB! ONLY IN AMERICA COULD I GET A JOB!"

WOO-HOO!

WHEN HOMER ARRIVES AT THE BOUVIER HOUSE TO TELL MARGE THE GOOD NEWS, HE LEARNS SHE WENT INTO LABOR HOURS EARLIER.

"COME ON. I'LL DRIVE."

MAN OF THE HOUSE

WITH NEWFOUND CONFIDENCE, HOMER RUSHES TO TELL MARGE ABOUT HIS NEW JOB.

"Starting tomorrow, I'm a nuclear technician."
—HOMER

"God help us!"
—DR. HIBBERT

UNFORTUNATELY, HE MIGHT BE A LITTLE TOO CONFIDENT.

"STEP ASIDE. I'LL DELIVER THIS BABY!"

"WHY DON'T YOU LET ME HANDLE THIS?"

SOON, MARGE GIVES BIRTH TO A BOUNCING BABY BOY.

"ISN'T HE BEAUTIFUL?"

"AS LONG AS HE'S GOT EIGHT FINGERS AND EIGHT TOES, HE'S FINE BY ME."

-HOMER

BABY'S PREMIERE PRANK

BART IS ONLY TEN MINUTES OLD BEFORE HE GETS HIS HANDS ON HOMER'S LIGHTER.

"AH, BART. DADDY'S LITTLE ANGEL."

–HOMER

FIRE IN THE HOLE!

HOMER'S NONE TOO PLEASED WITH THE RESULTS.

"WHY, YOU LITTLE....!"

"HE DID THAT ON PURPOSE!"

EAST SIDE STORY

WITH BABY IN TOW, THE YOUNG PARENTS MOVE INTO AN APARTMENT IN SPRINGFIELD'S LOWER EAST SIDE.

"LOOK, BART, IT'S DADDY."

"HOMER!"

"THAT'S WHAT GROWN-UPS CALL ME, SON. SAY, 'DADDY.'"

"HOMER!"

"DA-DEE."

IT'S A TIME FULL OF POTENTIAL...

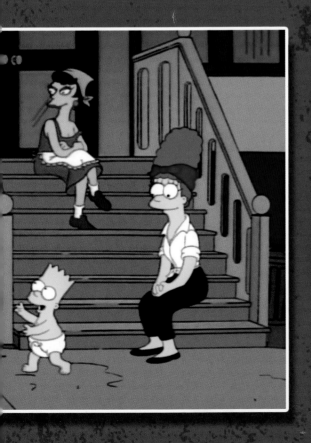

"HO-MER!"

"WHY, YOU LITTLE...!"

...AND QUESTIONABLE PARENTING.

WILD CHILD

BUT THE TWO SOON LEARN THAT
BABY BART IS EVEN MORE RAMBUNCTIOUS
THAN THEY BARGAINED FOR.

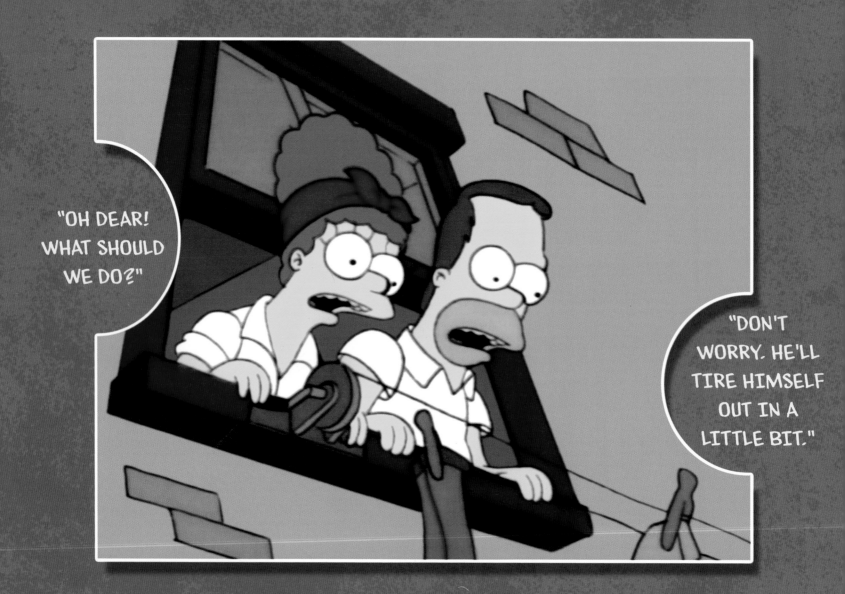

"OH DEAR! WHAT SHOULD WE DO?"

"DON'T WORRY. HE'LL TIRE HIMSELF OUT IN A LITTLE BIT."

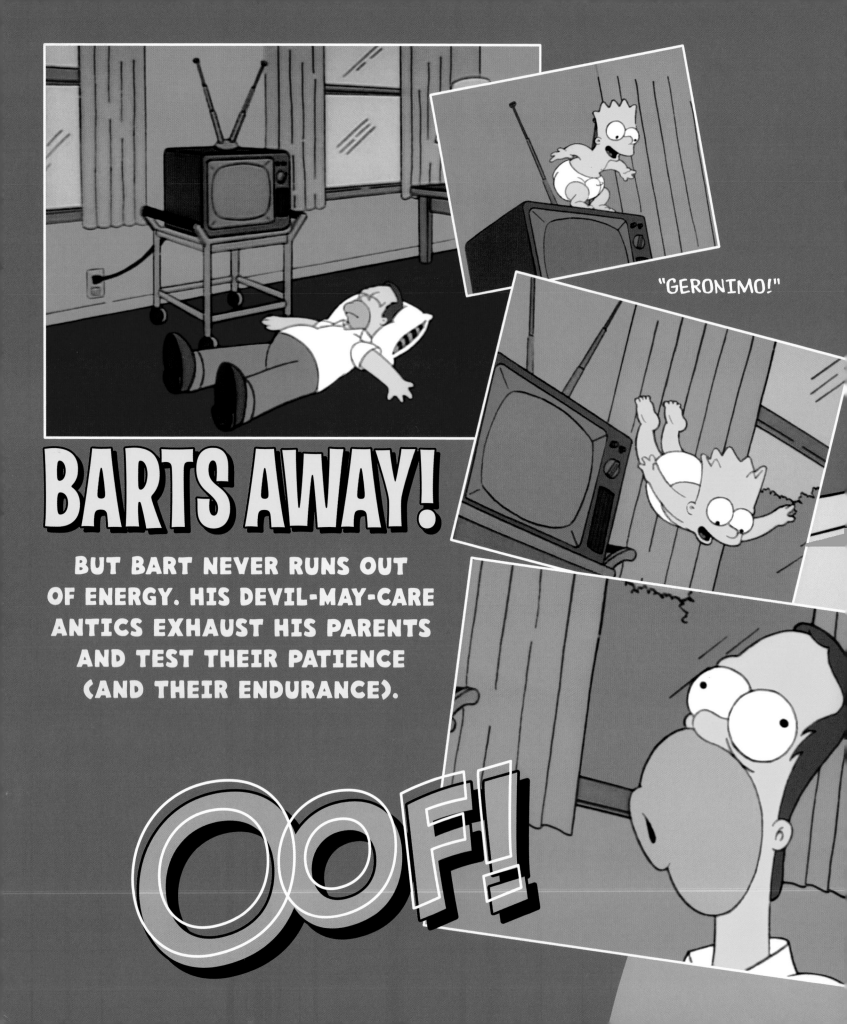

BARTS AWAY!

BUT BART NEVER RUNS OUT OF ENERGY. HIS DEVIL-MAY-CARE ANTICS EXHAUST HIS PARENTS AND TEST THEIR PATIENCE (AND THEIR ENDURANCE).

"GERONIMO!"

OOF!

LIKE FATHER,

MARGE HAS HER HANDS FULL WITH TAKING CARE OF A MESSY, STINKY BABY.

LIKE SON...

FORTUNATELY, SHE'S HAD A LOT OF PRACTICE.

BART'S FIRST WORD

"RAISING A KID IS HARD...UNTIL WE FIGURED OUT WE COULD JUST SIT HIM IN FRONT OF THE TV."

—HOMER

IN SEARCH OF ENTERTAINMENT, BART STEALS INTO HIS PARENTS' ROOM...

"HOMER, YOU FORGOT TO LOCK THE DOOR."

First Anniversary

MARGE AND HOMER CELEBRATE ONE YEAR OF MARRIAGE WITH A TRIP TO THE TOWNE CENTRE AT SPRINGFIELDE GLENNE (WHICH IS A FANCY WAY OF SAYING "THE MALL").

"OUR FIRST ANNIVERSARY. AND WE'RE MORE IN LOVE THAN EVER."
—MARGE

"IN YOUR FACE, PEOPLE WHO SAID IT WOULDN'T LAST A YEAR!"
—HOMER

RAISING A CHILD HAS TAKEN A TOLL ON THEIR LOVE LIFE. THEY NEVER HAVE A MINUTE TO THEMSELVES.

BART GETS FRIENDLY WITH A MANNEQUIN
FROM COSTINGTON'S DEPARTMENT STORE.

EVEN STOLEN KISSES ARE CUT SHORT BY THE JEERS OF LAUGHING SHOPPERS.

...WITH
MIXED RESULTS.

"Moustache daddy good.
Fat daddy smell like beer!"
—BABY BART

MARGE AND HOMER TAKE A SPIN ON THE MALL TRAIN RIDE,
WHICH FOREVER AFTER BECOMES A SYMBOL OF THEIR LOVE.

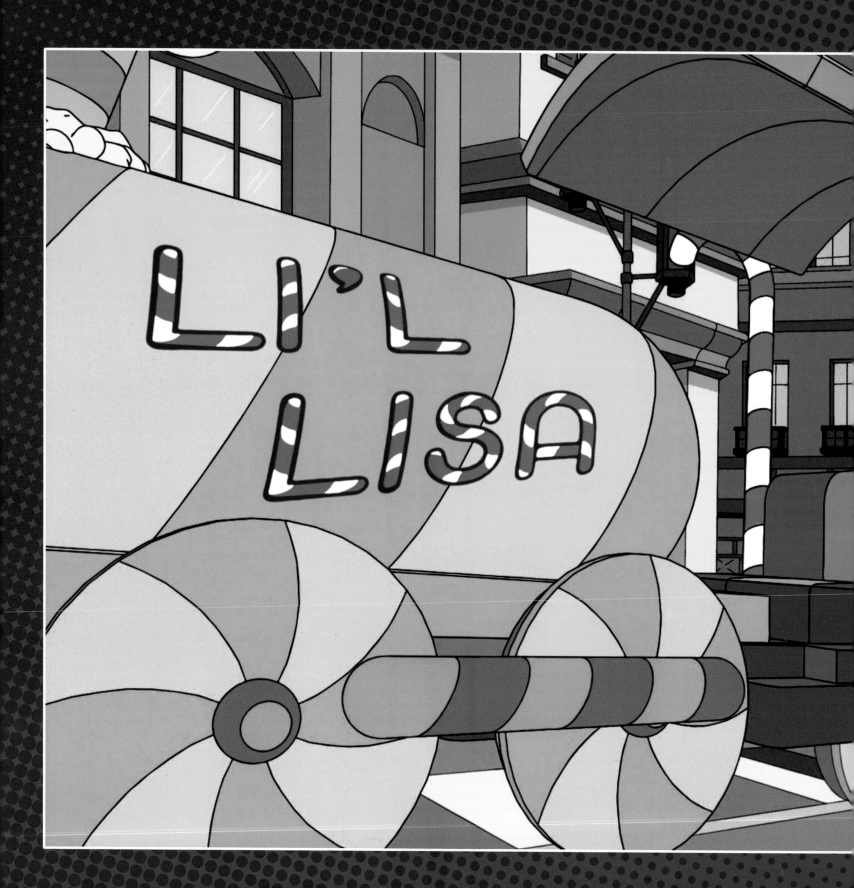

NOT ONLY DOES THE TRAIN ALLOW THE TWO LOVEBIRDS TIME FOR SOME "RELAXATION," IT'S ALSO THE INSPIRATION BEHIND THEIR NEW DAUGHTER'S NAME.

"WAIT... YOU'RE SAYING I WAS NAMED AFTER A TRAIN?"
—LISA

"YEAH, JUST LIKE WE DID WITH BART."
—HOMER

BART APPEARS IN THE "BABY STINK-BREATH" COMMERCIAL

OPEN: A BEAUTIFUL DAY IN THE PARK...

BABY: (EVIL GIGGLE)

(JINGLE)

He's The Baby Whose Mouth Smells Like Death Run For Your Life It's Baby Stink-Breath!

(V.O.) ...WHILE LEAVING THE RNA UNTOUCHED!

OLD WOMAN: NO MORE BABY STINK-BREATH!

OLD WOMAN: WHAT A BEAUTIFUL BABY...

OLD WOMAN: (GASP!) WHAT HORRIBLE BREATH!

MOM: I'LL JUST USE THE
BABY-SO-FRESH TRI-PATCH SYSTEM!

(V.O.) THESE SOOTHING CHEMICALS
ALTER YOUR BABY'S DNA...

BABY: (HAPPY LAUGH)

(V.O.) NOT SAFE FOR BABIES UNDER TWO.

A PREGNANT PAUSE

MARGE SHARES SOME WONDERFUL NEWS WITH HER HUSBAND.

YAAAAHHHH!!

HE DOESN'T TAKE IT AS WELL AS SHE HAD HOPED.

Homer:0 | Hair Loss:2

THE GANGSTER'S PARADISE

CAT LOVER'S HIDEAWAY

RENDERING PLANT ADJACENT

"OH DEAR!"

"ACTUALLY, THE CATS OWN THE HOUSE. YOU'D BE THEIR TENANT."

"ONCE YOU GET USED TO THE SMELL OF MELTED HOG FAT, YOU'LL WONDER HOW YOU EVER DID WITHOUT IT."

"MMMM...HOG FAT."

THE HUNT CONTINUES

HOMER AND MARGE EVEN CONSIDER THE POSSIBILITY OF BUYING A HOUSEBOAT...

"DON'T FORGET TO CHECK OUT THE GALLEY. THAT'S REAL SHAG CARPETING."

...BUT THEY'RE NOT TOO KEEN ON THE NEIGHBORS.

EVENTUALLY, THEY FIND A HOUSE THAT FITS THEM PERFECTLY.

"OH, HOMER, JUST IMAGINE WHAT WE CAN DO TO THE PLACE!"

NOW IT'S SIMPLY A MATTER OF A LITTLE FINANCIAL WRANGLING.

UNABLE TO AFFORD THE DOWN PAYMENT, HOMER APPROACHES HIS DAD FOR HELP.

"DAD, I NEED $15,000 TO BUY A HOME."

ABE AGREES TO SELL HIS OWN HOUSE AND WRITE HOMER A CHECK.

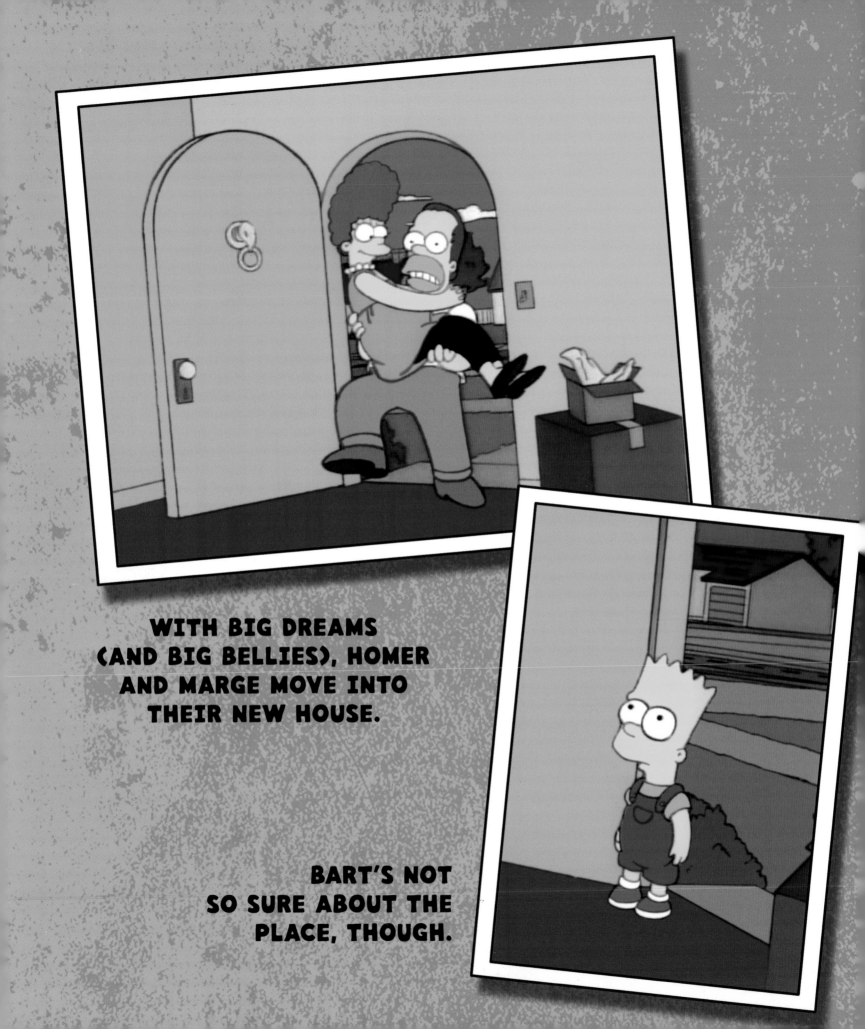

WITH BIG DREAMS
(AND BIG BELLIES), HOMER
AND MARGE MOVE INTO
THEIR NEW HOUSE.

BART'S NOT
SO SURE ABOUT THE
PLACE, THOUGH.

LOVE THY NEIGHBOR

IT'S NOT LONG BEFORE THEIR NEW NEIGHBOR, NED FLANDERS, STOPS BY FOR A VISIT.

"IF YOU NEED ANYTHING, JUST GIVE A WHISTLE."

BONUS TRIVIA | Q: WHAT IS THE FIRST ITEM HOMER BORROWS FROM NED?
A: A TV TRAY.

THE BIRTH OF LISA

ONE SIMPSON TOO MANY?

THE DAY ARRIVES AND MARGE
DELIVERS A HEALTHY BABY GIRL.

EVERYONE IS OVER THE MOON FOR THIS LITTLE BUNDLE OF JOY.

BART WORRIES THAT LISA WILL STEAL AWAY HIS PARENTS' TIME AND ATTENTION...

...AND FOR GOOD REASON.

"WHAT?"

MARGE TAKES THE KIDS
TO SEE HER SISTERS.

PATTY AND SELMA ARE
SMITTEN WITH THE NEW BABY.

WATCH
OUT
FOR
AUNTS!

BUT FOR LISA,
THE WHOLE
EXPERIENCE
IS A LITTLE
HAIR-RAISING.

"I'M GONNA GIVE
HER A KISS."

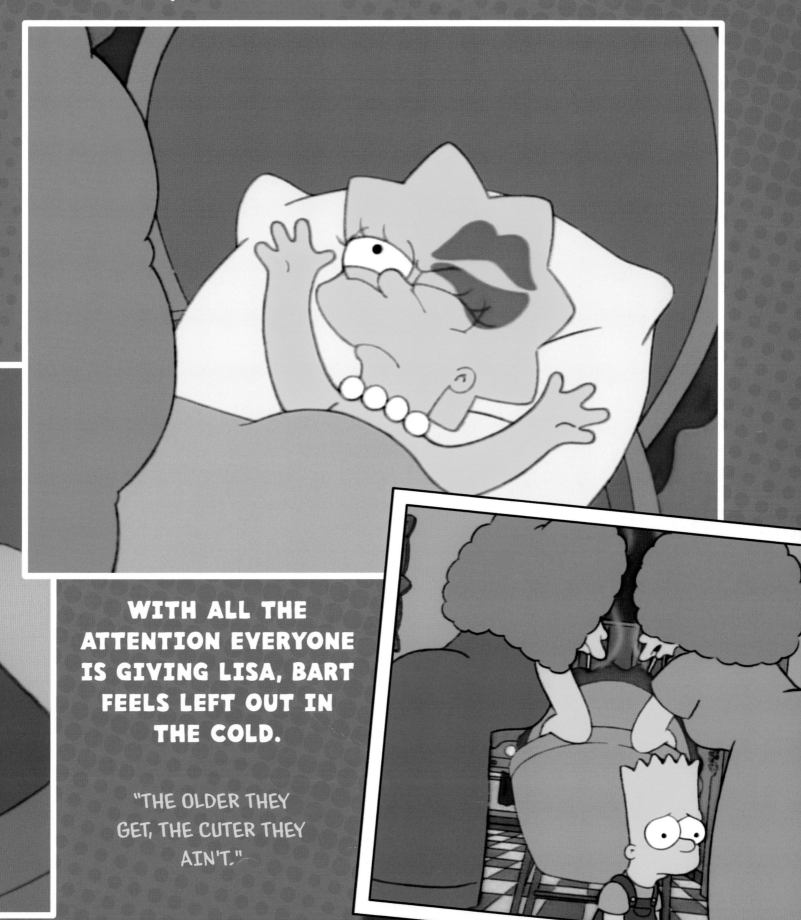

STILL, SHE MANAGES TO MUDDLE THROUGH.

WITH ALL THE ATTENTION EVERYONE IS GIVING LISA, BART FEELS LEFT OUT IN THE COLD.

"THE OLDER THEY GET, THE CUTER THEY AIN'T."

IF YOU SHOULD DIE BEFORE

BART IS RELUCTANT TO GIVE UP HIS CRIB FOR THE NEW BABY, SO HOMER PROMISES TO BUILD HIM HIS OWN BED.

YOU WAKE...
"SEE? IT'S A CLOWN. EVERYONE LOVES CLOWNS!"
-HOMER
"MUST...NOT...SLEEP. CLOWN'LL...EAT ME."
-BART

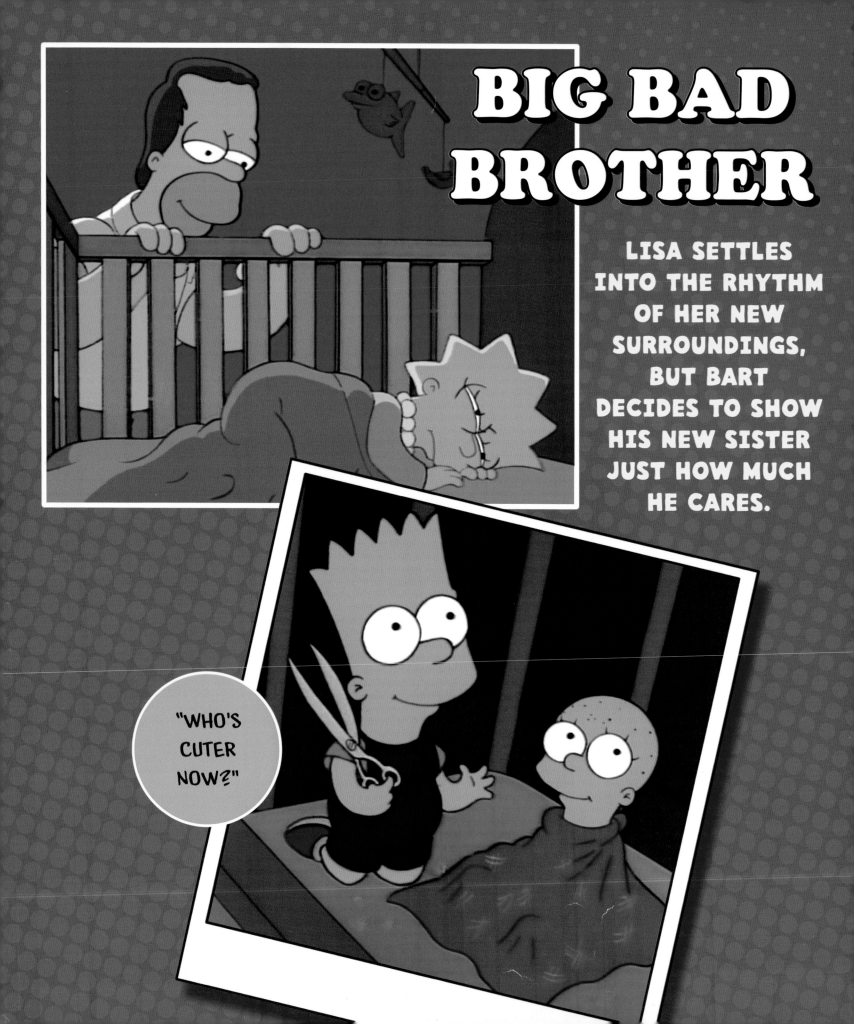

BIG BAD BROTHER

LISA SETTLES INTO THE RHYTHM OF HER NEW SURROUNDINGS, BUT BART DECIDES TO SHOW HIS NEW SISTER JUST HOW MUCH HE CARES.

"WHO'S CUTER NOW?"

THIS LANDS HIM IN HOT WATER WITH HIS PARENTS, BUT BABY LISA JUST CAN'T GET ENOUGH OF HER BIG BROTHER.

STILL, BART IS UNDETERRED FROM GETTING RID OF THE LITTLE PEST.

DESPITE BART'S BEST EFFORTS, LISA REMAINS HAPPY AND HEALTHY.

"LISA'S JUST FINE. SHE HAS THE REFLEXES OF A YOUNG MARY LOU RETTON."

THE SAME CAN'T BE SAID FOR HOMER.

"BOY, GET YOUR BUTT IN THE CORNER AND STAY THERE."

DON'T DO THE CRIME IF YOU CAN'T DO THE TIME

BART BECOMES MORE OR LESS A PERMANENT
FIXTURE IN THE "TIME-OUT ZONE."

UNABLE TO STOMACH ANY MORE, BART DECIDES TO RUN AWAY.

"I LIKED IT WHEN IT WAS ME, MOM, AND HOMER. YOU WRECKED EVERYTHING. I'M LEAVING!"

HE TRIES TO ESCAPE THE HOUSE, BUT HE CAN'T ESCAPE

LISA'S FIRST WORD

BART!

"WHAT DID YOU JUST SAY?"

AND THEN, THE FLOODGATES OPEN...

BART! BART! BART!

"SUFFERIN' SUCCOTASH! YOU CAN TALK! I'M YOUR FIRST WORD!"

"WELL, I'M NOT SURPRISED. LISA'S CRAZY ABOUT YOU. SHE THINKS YOU HUNG THE MOON!"

REALIZING HE'S BEEN WRONG ABOUT HIS LITTLE SISTER, BART RESOLVES TO BE THE BEST BROTHER EVER.

IT'S A RESOLUTION THAT LASTS FOR ABOUT 12 SECONDS.

MUSIC SOOTHES THE SAVAGE BEAST

AS A MEANS OF RELAXATION, HOMER TURNS ONCE AGAIN TO MUSIC. HE STARTS A BARBERSHOP QUARTET WITH SOME FRIENDS AND EVEN RELEASES A FEW ALBUMS.

"ROCK 'N' ROLL HAD BECOME STAGNANT. 'ACHY BREAKY HEART' WAS SEVEN YEARS AWAY. SOMETHING HAD TO FILL THE VOID, AND THAT SOMETHING WAS BARBERSHOP."

—HOMER

THE "BE SHARPS" SOON BECOME INCREDIBLY POPULAR AND ARE CALLED UPON TO PERFORM THROUGHOUT THE NATION.

MARGE DOES HER BEST TO KEEP BART AND LISA FROM FORGETTING THEIR ABSENT FATHER, BUT HER EFFORTS FALL FLAT.

THE RELENTLESS TOURING SOON TAKES ITS TOLL ON THE BAND MEMBERS.

TEMPERS FLARE AND HARSH WORDS ARE EXCHANGED.

"HOMER, THIS SONG IS WORSE THAN THE ONE YOU WROTE ABOUT MR. T!"
—APU

ONCE BARNEY BEGINS
DATING A JAPANESE CONCEPTUAL
ARTIST, THINGS TAKE A TURN
FOR THE WORSE.

"ARE WE HOT?"

–HOMER

THE FINAL STRAW
COMES WHEN THE
GROUP IS NAMED IN
"US" MAGAZINE'S
ANNUAL "WHAT'S HOT
AND WHAT'S NOT"
ISSUE.

"NO, WE ARE NOT."

–PRINCIPAL SKINNER

THE BAND GOES THEIR
SEPARATE WAYS, AND HOMER
FINDS HIMSELF BACK AT
THE POWER PLANT WHERE
HE MAKES USE OF HIS
PROBLEM-SOLVING SKILLS.

WE BREAK DOWN
HOMER'S DISAPPEARING HAIRLINE

HAIR THAT'S FLOWING.

NOW IT'S GOING...

...GOING...

...GONE!

A MOTHER'S PRIDE

MARGE SUBMITS A FAMILY PHOTO AND IS ELATED WHEN IT'S CHOSEN FOR THE COVER OF THE SPRINGFIELD PHONE BOOK.

"ISN'T IT CUTE? AND IT'LL
BE IN EVERY HOUSE IN THE CITY!"
-MARGE

NOPE, NOTHING EMBARRASSING ABOUT THAT!

FINANCIAL FREEDOM

AFTER EIGHT YEARS OF WORKING AT THE POWER PLANT, HOMER FINALLY EARNS ENOUGH MONEY TO PAY OFF HIS DEBT.

"WITH THIS SINGLE GLORIOUS CHECK, I'M FINALLY COMPLETELY OUT OF DEBT."

"WITH MY BILLS PAID OFF, I CAN FINALLY QUIT THIS LOUSY JOB!"

HE BIDS FAREWELL TO HIS BUDDIES AND MOVES ON TO THE NEXT PHASE...

"DID YOU HEAR ME? I SAID I QUIT, MONTY!"

SINCE HE'S QUITTING, HOMER DECIDES HE CAN DO ANYTHING HE FEELS LIKE.

"WHAT ARE YOU DOING? STOP THIS INSTANT!"

SOON, HOMER PURSUES HIS

DREAM

SINCE HIS PAL BARNEY ALREADY WORKS THERE, HOMER ASKS HIM TO ACT AS AN INTERMEDIARY.

"HEY, UNCLE AL.
CAN HOMER HAVE A JOB?"

JOB IN PARADISE.

THE PARADISE OF THE BOWLING ALLEY, THAT IS.

"SURE."

"BARNEY, YOU'RE FIRED."

DATE NIGHT

TO CELEBRATE HIS NEW JOB, HOMER TAKES MARGE OUT
FOR AN EVENING OF DINING AND DANCING...

...WHICH CONSISTS OF DRIVE-THRU
AT KRUSTY BURGER AND LISTENING TO THE
RADIO. THAT'S THE BEST HE CAN AFFORD
ON A PIN MONKEY'S SALARY.

THEY TAKE A
STROLL ON THE
BEACH...

LATER THAT EVENING, HOMER SHARES HIS HOPES FOR THE FUTURE.

"EVERYTHING IN OUR LIVES IS EXACTLY, PERFECTLY BALANCED. I HOPE THINGS STAY THIS WAY FOREVER."

My Father, THE PIN MONKEY

AS HOMER BEGINS HIS NEW CAREER AT THE BOWLARAMA, HE QUICKLY MASTERS EACH OF HIS NEW DUTIES.

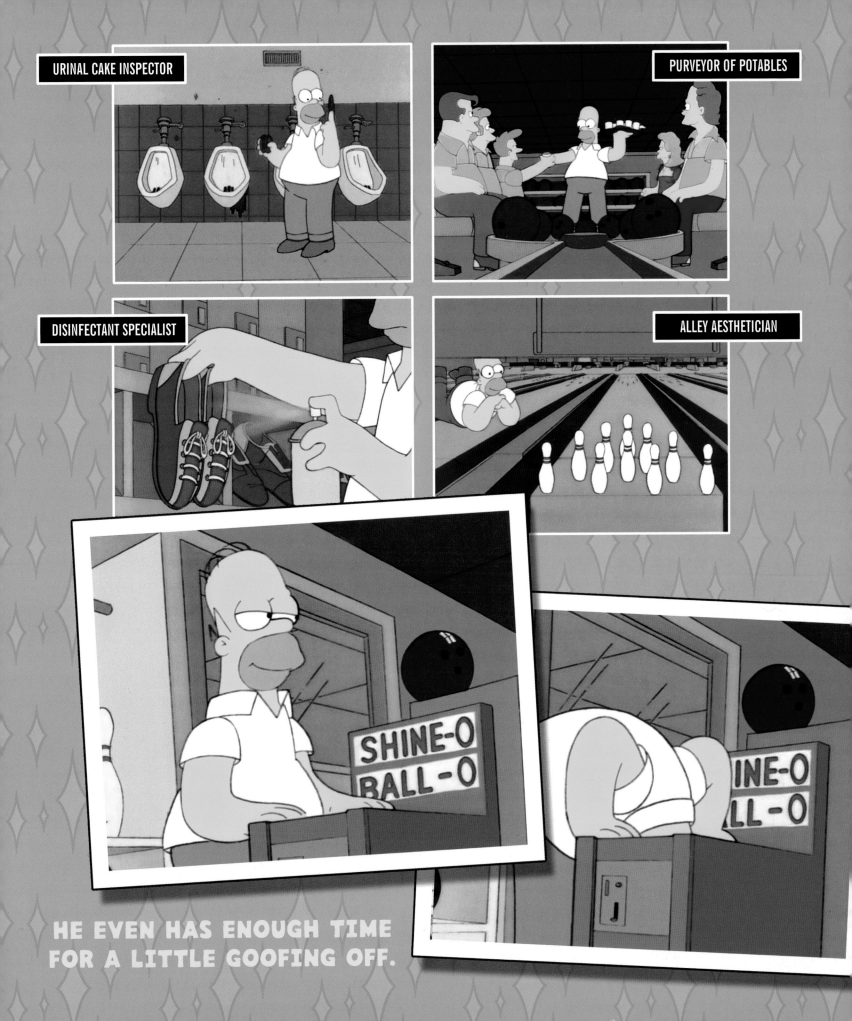

The Best Laid Plans...

"HEY! YOU HOG THE BATHROOM EVERY MORNING. I HAVE TO WASH MY HAIR!"

A FEW WEEKS LATER, THINGS BEGIN TO CHANGE.

A CONCERNED MARGE PAYS A VISIT TO DR. HIBBERT.

"CONGRATULATIONS, MRS. SIMPSON. YOU'RE PREGNANT."

MARGE IS HAPPY TO TELL BART AND LISA
ABOUT THEIR IMPENDING SIBLING...

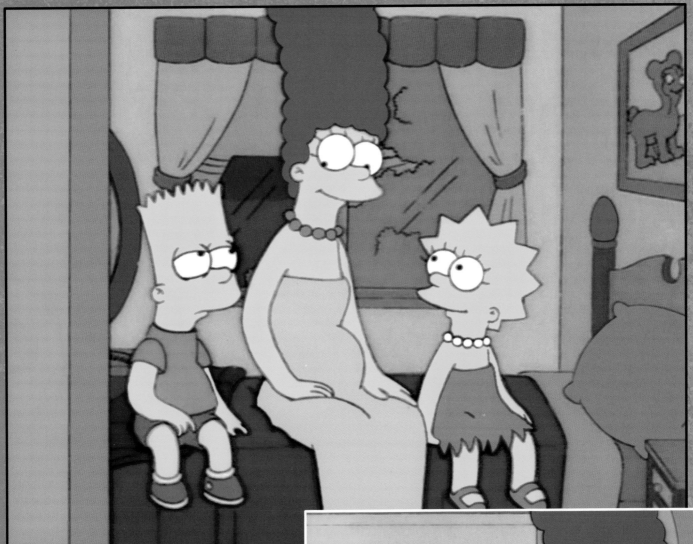

"BEEN THERE, DONE THAT."

—BART

...BUT SHE WORRIES HOW HOMER WILL REACT.

OOOOOOO!!!

HOMER GOES INTO PANIC MODE WHENEVER HE THINKS ABOUT ANOTHER MOUTH TO FEED.

"ALL OUR FINANCIAL PLANS ARE RUINED. WE'RE DOOMED! DOOMED, I TELLS YA!"

HOMER REALIZES THE ONLY WAY HE CAN STAY AT THE BOWLING ALLEY IS TO INCREASE BUSINESS SO HE CAN GET A RAISE.

HE POURS ALL HIS ENERGIES INTO TRIPLING THE BUSINESS.

AFTER HOURS OF WORK HE FINALLY COMES UP WITH A MASTER PLAN!

"OF COURSE!"

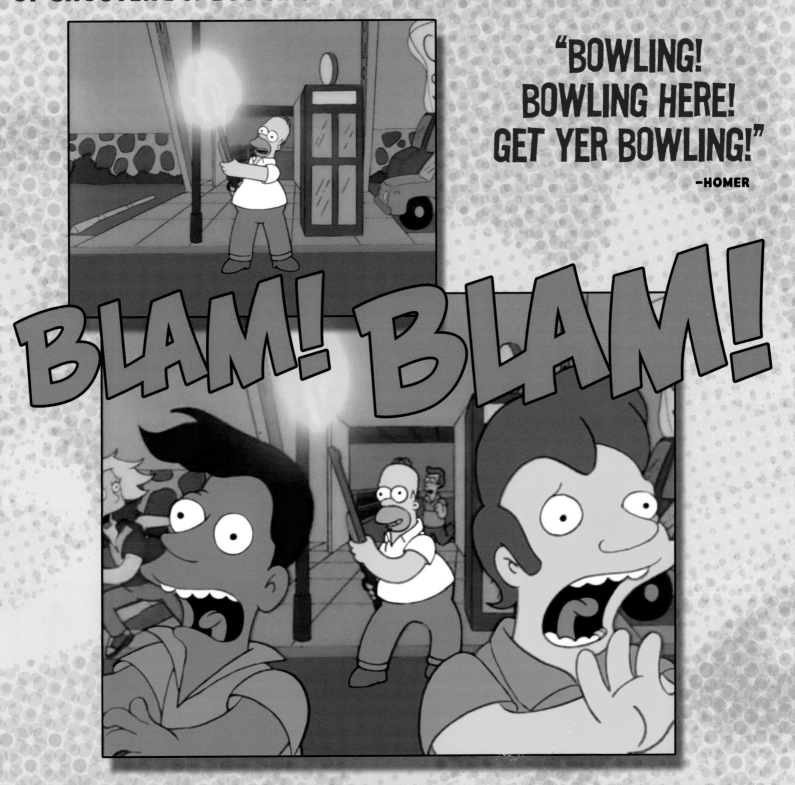

WITH HIS PLAN A COMPLETE FAILURE AND POLICE CHARGES NARROWLY AVOIDED, HOMER RETREATS TO THE LANES FOR ONE LAST LOOK BEFORE HE QUITS HIS DREAM JOB.

"WE'RE REALLY GONNA MISS YOU, HOMER. THE PLACE HAS NEVER BEEN CLEANER, AND THE WAY YOU KEPT THE YOUNG PEOPLE AWAY...THAT WAS BEAUTIFUL."

"WE ALL PITCHED IN AND WE GOT YOU THIS LITTLE GOING-AWAY PRESENT."

HOMER NEEDS MORE MONEY TO SUPPORT HIS GROWING FAMILY, SO HE LEAVES THE BOWLARAMA AND HEADS TO THE ONE PLACE IN TOWN WHERE A GUY LIKE HIM CAN EARN THAT KIND OF INCOME...

...THE SPRINGFIELD NUCLEAR POWER PLANT.

(CUE DRAMATIC MUSIC)

SUPPLICANTS

SWALLOWING HIS PRIDE, HOMER RETURNS TO MR. BURNS AND BEGS FOR HIS OLD JOB.

"SO, YOU'VE COME CRAWLING BACK, EH?"

"SEEMS LIKE THE CLASSY THING TO DO WOULD BE NOT TO CALL ATTENTION TO IT."

MR. BURNS GIVES HOMER HIS JOB BACK ON ONE CONDITION...

"AS PUNISHMENT FOR YOUR DESERTION, IT'S COMPANY POLICY TO GIVE YOU THE PLAGUE."

—MR. BURNS

"AH, SIR... I THINK YOU MEAN 'THE PLAQUE.'"

—MR. SMITHERS

TO BREAK WHAT'S LEFT OF HIS SPIRIT, HOMER IS FORCED TO SPEND EVERY WORKDAY LOOKING AT THE SPECIAL DEMOTIVATIONAL PLAQUE THAT MR. BURNS HAS INSTALLED.

DON'T FORGET: YOU'RE HERE FOREVER.

AND MAGGIE MAKES THREE

SPRINGFIELD
GENERAL HOSPITAL

"IF A SURGEON LEAVES
SOMETHING IN YOU,
IT'S YOURS!"

ON MARGE'S DELIVERY
DAY, HOMER MAKES ALL THE
RIGHT NOISES, BUT HIS HEART'S
JUST NOT IN IT.

"OH BOY. IT'S WONDERFUL. IT'S MAGICAL.
HERE IT COMES, ANOTHER MOUTH..."

WHEN THE BABY GETS THE OKAY FROM THE DOCTOR, HOMER GIVES A RELUCTANT THUMBS-UP.

"HOMIE, I THINK SOMEONE IS SAYING HELLO."

AND IN AN INSTANT, HE FALLS HEAD OVER HEELS FOR MAGGIE.

"AW, MARGE, WE HAVE A WONDERFUL BABY GIRL. AND NOT JUST A GIRL. THE MOST BEAUTIFUL BABY GIRL IN THE WHOLE WORLD."

HOMER MAY BE
STUCK WORKING
AT THE POWER
PLANT FOR THE
REST OF HIS DAYS,
BUT MAGGIE IS
THERE WITH HIM
EVERY STEP OF
THE WAY.

THE LAST PIECE OF THE PUZZLE

HOMER TAKES BART TO THE DOG TRACK IN A LAST-DITCH EFFORT TO WIN SOME MONEY FOR THE FAMILY'S CHRISTMAS GIFTS.

HE PUTS EVERYTHING ON A 99:1 LONG SHOT BY THE NAME OF "SANTA'S LITTLE HELPER." THE DOG COMES IN DEAD LAST.

"GET LOST! YOU CAME IN LAST FOR THE LAST TIME! DON'T COME BACK!"

HOMER RELUCTANTLY AGREES TO RESCUE THE ABANDONED POOCH.

"HEY, EVERYBODY! LOOK WHAT WE GOT!"

EVERYONE IS OVERJOYED WITH HOMER'S GIFT, AND THE SIMPSON FAMILY IS FINALLY COMPLETE.

SIMPSON FAMILY FUN FACT!

SECRET SIBLINGS

A CARNIVAL WORKER ONCE SEDUCED ABE SIMPSON WITH A GAME OF "DUNK THE CLOWN." ONE YEAR LATER, SHE RETURNED WITH A NEWBORN IN TOW.

"SHE DID THINGS YOUR MOTHER WOULD NEVER DO...LIKE HAVE SEX FOR MONEY."

—ABE

THE BABY WAS LEFT AT THE SPRINGFIELD ORPHANAGE AND LATER ADOPTED. HE GREW UP TO BECOME...

HERB POWELL
MILLIONAIRE INVENTOR AND AUTO INDUSTRY MOGUL

IN HIS ENLISTED DAYS, ABE COURTED A LOCAL GIRL WHILE STATIONED IN ENGLAND.

"EDWINA, MY SLOWLY OPENING FLOWER, I'M SHIPPING OUT IN THE MORNING. WON'T YOU MAKE MY LAST NIGHT MEMORABLE?"

MANY DECADES LATER, HOMER MEETS THE RESULT OF THEIR STEAMY TRYST.

"LADY, YOU'RE GORGEOUS! YOU MAKE DAME EDNA LOOK LIKE A DUDE!"

IT'S NOT EASY BEING HOMER

MYSTERIES OF SPRINGFIELD

WHO IS BARTO?

IS HE VANDAL OR VAN GOGH? LITTLE IS KNOWN ABOUT THIS SECRETIVE STREET ARTIST, BUT HIS HANDIWORK CAN BE FOUND ON MANY OF THE CITY'S LOCAL LANDMARKS, FROM THE BACK ALLEY OF BARNEY'S BOWLARAMA TO THE EMERGENCY EXIT OF THE AZTEC THEATER.

THE MANY OCCUP

GRAMMY WINNER

THE CHOSEN ONE

SAFETY SALAMANDER

TOWN CRIER

ATIONS OF HOMER

PAPARAZZO

SEASONAL SANTA

G.I. D'OH!

VILLAGE PEOPLE ENTHUSIAST

EVEN MORE THE MANY OCCUP

POPSICLE PUSHER

UNDERCOVER OPERATIVE

FIREMAN (NON-SEXY)

BEACON OF ENLIGHTENMENT

ATIONS OF HOMER

TASTE TESTER

ANGER MANAGEMENT

HIS MAJESTY

CIVIL WAR REENACTOR

THE WRITE STUFF

REALIZING THAT HE'S NEVER SEEN SOMEONE
LIKE HIMSELF ON TELEVISION, HOMER TRIES HIS HAND
AT WRITING A TV SHOW. HE CREATES A MORE REALISTIC
PROGRAM AND BASES IT ON HIS FAMILY...

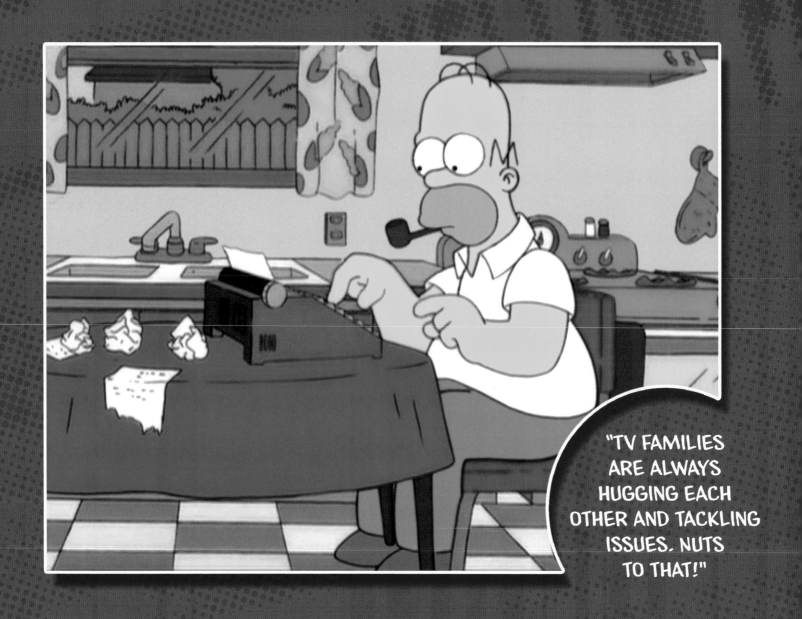

"TV FAMILIES
ARE ALWAYS
HUGGING EACH
OTHER AND TACKLING
ISSUES. NUTS
TO THAT!"

...WHO HE RECRUITS AS HIS CAST.

"THIS MAKEUP BETTER BE CRUELTY-FREE!"

ACTING AS WRITER, PRODUCER, DIRECTOR, AND STAR, HOMER FILMS A LOW-BUDGET VIDEO IN HIS HOME.

WITH HIS FIVE-MINUTE PILOT IN TOW, THIS FLEDGLING FELLINI TAKES THE NEXT STEP...

LIFE'S A PITCH

...AND TAKES HIS IDEA TO HOLLYWOOD, WHERE IT'S QUICKLY OPTIONED BY THE FOX NETWORK.

HOMER SIGNS A THIRTEEN-EPISODE CONTRACT, AND FILMING BEGINS IMMEDIATELY.

NOTICING THE SIMPSONS HAVE REAL-WORLD CHEMISTRY, THE NETWORK CASTS THE REST OF THE FAMILY IN THE NEW SERIES.

"DAD, I'VE NEVER SAID 'COWABUNGA' IN MY LIFE. YOUR SCRIPT SUCKS."
—BART

NO SOONER DOES THE FIRST EPISODE AIR THAN EVERYONE REALIZES THE SIMPSONS SHOW IS A SMASH HIT...

DAILY VARIETY

YELLOW FEVER

THE HOLLYWOOD REPORTER

BUMPTIOUS BROOD BOFFO

...AND THE REST IS HISTORY.